2 Manuscripts:

EMOTIONAL INTELLIGENCE:

How to Become a Lively And Likeable Leader

LEADERSHIP

How To Make Difficult Co-Workers Respect,
Admire And Follow You

by Samuel Yildiz

DISCLAIMER

The information in this book is presented for purposes of education and information only. The author is in no way liable for any outcomes sustained by the reader as the direct or indirect result of the implementation of any advice contained herein. If you know or suspect that you require professional help, for example in overcoming psychological difficulties, you must consult with a suitably-qualified person.

Contents

Chapter I:

Why Emotional Intelligence Is More Important Than Rational Thinking

What Is Emotional Intelligence?

Do you know someone who is good at managing their emotions? Someone who is good at expressing their thoughts, hopes and even their most personal feelings in a clear, appropriate manner? Someone who is great at handling other peoples' emotions, even during awkward moments? If so, then this person is emotionally intelligent.

If you are emotionally intelligent, you are the master of your own feelings. You know how to survive a bad mood without it ruining your day, and you know how to use your emotional energy wisely. If your EQ (Emotional Quotient – a measure of emotional intelligence) is high, then you know exactly how to ride out even the worst stuff life throws at you with your sanity and dignity intact.

For a long time, traditional intelligence – what we refer to as 'intelligence quotient' or 'IQ' – was seen as the only kind of intelligence worth bothering with. Someone with a high IQ is usually good at tasks like solving logic puzzles and solving equations. If you've ever taken an IQ test, you'll know that they measure these kinds of mental abilities but ignore skills relating to emotions and relationships.

However, over the past 30 years or so, psychologists have begun to realize that traditional ideas about intelligence have overlooked a key part of human experience - emotion. In the 1990s, the phrase 'emotional intelligence' appeared on the psychology scene when it was used by Peter Salovey and John Mayer in their academic paper entitled 'Emotional Intelligence.' Since then, the idea of emotional intelligence has influenced not only psychologists but also teachers, business experts, entrepreneurs, and the millions of ordinary people who have read books on the subject.

Just as people vary in how good they are at solving math problems and other skills traditionally associated with 'being smart,' they also vary in how skilled they are in handling their own feelings and the feelings of others. Some people seem naturally able to remain calm and balanced. They accept a full range of emotions both in themselves and others. Other, however, people struggle to remain in control of themselves. The good news is that you can become more emotionally intelligent if you take the time to learn a few techniques and make some changes to your attitude.

In their landmark paper, Salovey and Mayer defined emotional intelligence in the following way: '...the ability to monitor one's own and others' feelings and emotions, to discriminate among them and to use this information to guide one's thinking and actions.' This is the definition that we will work with in this book.

Benefits Of Mastering Emotional Intelligence

If you think that emotional intelligence sounds useful, you are right. Let's take a look at exactly why improving your EQ is a smart investment of your time and effort. Remember that it takes time to make changes, but the research suggests that it will be worth it. Psychologists have demonstrated that you can improve your EI. Researchers at the University of Central Lancashire in the UK have shown that it is indeed possible to boost EI abilities through conscious effort and correct training (Pool & Qualter, 2012). In their work with 66 university students from a range of disciplines, the authors found that simply teaching participants how we feel emotions, how they affect us, and how they can be managed – the type of information covered in this book – had a noticeable effect on their EI scores a few weeks later. The participants took part in a range of activities to stimulate their EI development, and these will be covered later in this book so that you too can benefit from these findings.

There's more good news – the very fact that you have taken the step of downloading and reading this book suggests that you are happy to look at your strengths and weaknesses. This means you have at least a basic sense of self-awareness, which will serve you well as a good starting point. You can look forward to developing this awareness over the coming days and weeks. It will have a direct effect on every area of your life.

The benefits of working on your EQ are as follows:

- Your personal relationships will improve.
If you have a high EQ, you will have the ability to empathize with others and understand what they are feeling. This will make you a very desirable friend and romantic partner. Your family bonds will also become stronger. You will even become more in-demand as a business associate and colleague.

- You will be able to handle setbacks with greater ease.
Once you learn how to handle your strongest emotions – fear, anger, etc. – you need not fear them, because you can be confident that they need not set you back or consume hours of your time. This enables you to live more boldly. As a result you may fail more often – but you will also maximise your chances of success at the same time!

- You have a greater chance at earning more money and having a comfortable retirement.

3

People high in emotional intelligence can restrain themselves when needed, motivate themselves whenever they want and need to, and are good at getting in touch with their true needs and desires. This means that they are more likely to do work that they enjoy, which in turns mean they gain higher job satisfaction and earn a better rate of pay. They are better able to take calculated risk in their careers, knowing that even if things don't work out, they are able to reflect and learn from the experience.

Companies are increasingly testing potential candidates' EQs alongside their IQs and work-related skills. This means that working on your EQ could directly increase your chances of landing that next job.

- Being emotionally intelligent makes you a great leader.
Employees respond well to a supervisor with a high EQ, because these leaders take the time to understand everyone's strengths, weaknesses, and feelings. Therefore, by developing your own emotional intelligence you become a more attractive candidate for leadership positions. Follow the tips in this book and you will naturally develop yourself as a lively and likeable leader in both social and professional settings.

In the leadership literature, it is generally accepted that there are two principle types or styles of leadership. As Canadian researchers Barling, Slater and Kelloway (2000) put it, you can be a transactional leader, or you can be a transformational leader. What's the difference? Well, if you lead with a transactional style, you are focused primarily on particular outcomes, and on rewarding and punishing those you manage. Transactional leaders tend to try to expend the least amount of effort possible on managing their team, and are not always fair towards all members of the team. They may show favouritism and may not be transparent in their practices.

Transformational leadership, which is currently the most favoured leadership style in the western world, is very different. Transformational leaders seek to inspire others by upholding company values in such a way that motivates those they supervise to achieve their potential. How does this relate to EI? Well, to enact successful transformational leadership, you need to be able to tune into the emotions of others and understand their wants, needs and difficulties. Transformational leaders see every person they work with as an individual worthy of respect and have the ability to remain open-minded to the possibility that they will be challenged by opposing points of view and even rigorous conflict on occasion. They inspire trust and confidence in their subordinates, and tend to increase business performance into the bargain. To lead in this way, you need to be able to regulate your own emotions and deal with the stresses and challenges that will inevitably confront your team.

- Your daily interactions with everyone, from your partner to the bus driver, will be less stressful.

When you have a high EQ, you gain an understanding of other peoples' moods and motivations. This means that the communication between you and others will run smoothly, and you are less likely to be drawn into arguments or other negative interactions. You are less likely to do or say things that you later regret. This means fewer pointless debates, fewer fights, and less stress for everyone concerned!

- You will get more done at work, and in your leisure time.

People with high EQs have the ability to control their attention and stay focused for longer, which means that they are productive in their day-to-day lives. Imagine the effect this could have on your career! In addition, they also have the ability to contain any work stress or difficulties so that they do not intrude onto their personal time. Please note that emotionally intelligent people do not suppress all their emotions. This wouldn't be possible, and it even if it was, it wouldn't be healthy. However, those with high EQs do not allow their feelings to dominate their every waking moment.

- You will open yourself up to new experiences and appreciate another dimension of life.

When you start to work with and appreciate your emotions, you improve your understanding of what it is to be human. This will prime you to get more enjoyment out of meaningful books, movies, plays, and other media. You may even become inspired to create something of your own! This in turn can trigger a virtuous cycle, because exercising your creativity can make you more content and at ease with your emotions, which helps you feel less inhibited and freer to create...and so it continues.

- You will be healthier.

A higher EQ is linked with lower stress levels, greater levels of happiness, and better relationships. All these things are in turn related to good health. Moreover, those who are higher in EI are more likely to be able to deal with the difficult emotions that dealing with ill-health can bring. For example, emotional intelligence is linked to increased quality of life and wellbeing in patients with diabetes according to Turkish researchers (Yalcin et al., 2008). EI acts as a buffer between everyday stress and stress-related illnesses such as depression and chronic fatigue.

- Most of us think our EQs and IQs are higher than they really are, so even if you think your EQ is high, it could probably use some improvement.

Whether it's our driving skills or levels of honesty, most of us think that we are 'better' than the average person. This is also true for traditional and emotional intelligence. In other words, even if you think your EQ is fine, you might well be over-estimating it and it wouldn't hurt to work towards improving it! In a study of 260 people carried out by researchers from University College London, there was a positive but not absolute correlation between self-estimated and actual scores on tests of emotional intelligence (Petrides & Furnham, 2000). There is an important lesson here – do not believe that somebody is emotionally intelligent just because they say so. Even though most people have some degree of insight with regard to their own skill in this

6

area, it's important to still watch their interpersonal behaviour over time to see whether they really possess these abilities.

- If you have children, they will benefit when you improve your EQ.

Children learn their life skills from their parents. If you can model high-EQ behaviour for them, they are more likely to grow up possessing these skills, which in turn sets them up for a successful life.

- Mastering anything is in itself a great self-esteem boost!

Learning a new skill or improving yourself in some way will give you a shot of confidence, and that's never a bad thing.

You could even argue that EQ is more important than traditional IQ or the ability to think rationally. Why? Well, although certain intellectual skills are useful in a range of jobs and other situations, almost all of us have to navigate our social worlds every day. Being able to get on with others and manage yourself can open up a new world of opportunities.

The Negative Consequences Of A Low EQ

Let's look at the issue from another angle – what happens to people with low EQs? What, exactly, are the consequences of low emotional intelligence?

Essentially, if you fail to develop your EQ to the very best it can be, you are short-changing yourself of your best possible life. This sounds dramatic, but if you think about it you will soon realise that emotions and their management are essential to success in every area of life. If you consider a few everyday examples, you can see how this might play out.

Let's say you get into work one morning and your boss is standing by your desk looking concerned. What do you do? If you have a high EQ, you might not be happy to see your boss looking worried, but you would have an idea of how to handle the situation. You would use your existing knowledge of their personality, accurately assessing why they might be upset, and ask them what's wrong in a calm tone of voice. As a result, you would build your reputation as a good employee with great people skills.

Compare that to the reaction of a person with lower emotional intelligence. They might ask the boss an inappropriate question or even worse, fail to notice that the boss is upset in the first place! What do you think the consequences for this person's career would be?

Now consider an example that you may already come across in your personal life. Imagine that you have arrived at home early and are getting the dinner ready for your spouse or partner. Imagine that you are thinking about how pleased they will be to come home to a lovely meal.

However, the moment your partner gets in the door, you know your plan isn't going to work out. They come into the kitchen with a face that makes you think something must have gone seriously wrong. Worse, they barely seem to notice that you have put in so much effort into making them a nice meal. What do you do?

At this point, someone low in emotional intelligence would probably react badly. They would struggle to keep their emotions in check, thinking instead about how unfair it is that their partner was in a bad mood on that particular night. This negative attitude could then trigger an argument. Over time, this pattern of interaction can eat away at a previously strong relationship. In the worst-case scenario, some people end up repeating the same mistakes in more than one relationship, and never feel fully fulfilled in their personal lives.

On the other hand, someone with a high EQ would react very differently in this situation. They would recognise their own disappointment, but manage it to keep it to one side whilst they work out what is the matter with their partner. They would express concern, taking note of their partner's body language, facial expression, and their tone of voice. Someone high in EQ would understand that their partner couldn't possibly have known about the surprise dinner and that they are allowed to have occasional 'bad days.' They would make the effort to understand the reasons behind their partner's mood.

Which of theses two approaches do you think is likely to end well, and which in a nasty argument? Can you see why some people have made the argument that we ought to teach children and young people the skills needed to improve their emotional intelligence whilst they are still in school? Imagine how many misunderstandings could be avoided, how many relationships could be improved, if only we placed as much value on handling our feelings as we did developing skills such as mathematical reasoning and using correct sentence structure!

Rational Thinking And Its Limitations

If you're reading this book, you've probably been raised within a westernized culture. In the west, we prize 'rational thinking.' When you think rationally, the idea is that you see the world as it 'truly' is, and use logic rather than emotions when deciding what you ought to do next. In western cultures, emotions are often seen as less important. In fact, they are often seen as something only weak-minded people bother with! Most western people believe that you should 'think with your head' when making decisions, rather than 'listening to your heart.' This is a mistake, because emotions are real and important.

For example, suppose you are faced with a decision: You could take a new and better-paid job a few hundred miles away from your partner, or you could stay in the local area and take a less fulfilling job but have the opportunity to develop your relationship further. Logical, rational thinking is only going to take you so far in situations like this. You need to use some emotional intelligence to work out the true costs and benefits for everyone involved. Whatever the situation, there are always feelings to consider, both your own and those of other people. This is true whether in your personal life or even at work. If you are in a leadership role for example, you need to use your emotional intelligence to work out the best way to motivate, inspire and lead your team.

Ultimately, Emotions Should Lead The Way

You should now understand exactly why our emotions rather than just logical thinking 'drive the bus' in everyday life. Emotions shape every area of our lives, and so you should take every chance to develop your EQ. Sure, it's important to use your intellectual skills, abilities and willpower if you want to move ahead in your professional or personal life, but ultimately it's our emotions and how we react to them that shape our destinies.

How To Start Getting In Touch With Your Emotions Right Now

If you are feeling somewhat overwhelmed at the prospect of developing your EI, try the following two exercises to start you off. They do not require a huge amount of time or effort, and so are non-threatening paths to your own emotional development.

Exercise 1 – Keep A Journal
Buy a small notebook or set up a free digital journal online at Penzu (penzu.com). You don't have to become a committed diarist, but try to set aside a few minutes every day to record some general notes about how you are feeling. At first, you may find that the words don't come easily. You may even discover that your vocabulary isn't broad enough to allow you to capture your own feelings. This is a skill that can be developed in time and is valuable, because once you can describe your own emotions then you can start to evaluate them, record them, and communicate them to other people. If it helps, use a list of 'feelings words' to help you make your first few entries. Make a list of every possible emotion you can think of, and write them down. Now place a tick next to those that currently apply to you. If you can't think of many, run a quick Google search for 'Feelings lists' to find some useful free tools. Even if you can't manage to write anything else,

you are at least getting into the habit of tuning into your own feelings, which is a key element of developing your EI.

Exercise 2 – Go To A Gallery Or Play And Share The Experience With Others

Find a local art gallery or theatre and see a show or exhibition with at least one other person. During the experience, notice any feelings that arise within you. You might find this easy – for example, if you're watching a comedy and you're amused, there's nothing too tough about this exercise – but some emotions might not be so readily identified. If this happens, pay attention to your bodily cues. You may be watching a drama and unsure of how it makes you feel, but if you pay attention to your body, you may notice a slight tightening in your chest and nausea within your stomach. This may mean you feel scared or anxious in a way you cannot quite pin down. Don't try to push these feelings away. Welcome them as a chance to understand yourself better. Ask your companion how the art or performance makes them feel. By becoming accustomed to talking openly about your feeling with other people, you effortlessly begin to understand how others think and feel. Without even having to think about it, you will establish a reputation as a sensitive, caring friend, colleague and partner.

Chapter II:

What Are Emotions For?

Before we take a closer look at the mechanics of emotional intelligence and further explore techniques you can use to improve your EQ, let's take a few moments to go back to basics. We're going to look at what emotions actually are, and why we have them in the first place.

Emotions As A Survival Mechanism

What has ensured the survival of the human species thus far? Well, emotions have played a pretty big role! If your ancestors hadn't felt some strong emotions on a regular basis, you wouldn't be here to read this book.

Unless you managed to raise yourself, you were dependent on the emotional responses of other people for your survival. Imagine if your parents or guardians felt nothing for you, and weren't bothered as to whether you lived or died. Unable to fend for yourself, you would starve to death within a few days of birth! Thanks to the human capacity for emotions and inbuilt wish to bond with others (especially offspring), you made it through childhood.

Now consider your distant relative hunting on the savannah. His or her goals in life were quite simple: to live to adulthood, to find a suitable mate, to get enough food, and maybe even have a bit of fun along the way. The point is this: if this hypothetical ancestor is going to survive long enough to attain their goals, they have to survive. This is where emotion comes in.

A primary purpose of emotion is to detect threats and motivate the person feeling them to act accordingly. Imagine that your ancestor is out one day, perhaps gathering berries or setting a trap to catch an animal. Suddenly, a lion appears from behind a bush. Your ancestor promptly starts feeling terrified. This isn't a pleasant experience, but it has the useful side-effect of getting them to run away from the source of danger. They live to fight another day.

Emotions Don't Just Come From The Conscious Mind, Either

In the above example, it would be clear to the person in question why they were feeling scared. They know that they can see a lion. They know that the lion poses a threat. They know that in the face of this threat, they feel scared and so run away. You might not face down a hungry lion every day of your life, but you will be familiar with the modern equivalents: the cars that speed past you, the rowdy people outside bars near closing time, and so on. In the workplace, you'll be familiar with the rush of fear you might feel if your boss calls you into the office for an unexpected meeting, or the feeling of dread you get when a major client threatens to cancel their contract. By the way, being able to remember that everyone faces threats like this on a regular basis will make you naturally more empathic with regards to those around you. You are less likely to judge others harshly when you realise that everyone – and it has ever been so, since the beginning of the human species – is facing some kind of battle.

Not all emotions are obvious in how they present themselves. Some don't come from our conscious minds. Sometimes, they emerge from the unconscious. 'The unconscious' might sound like a piece of unnecessary jargon, but all it really means is 'the part of the mind we don't see or think about in our day-to-day life' or 'our deeper selves.'

Sigmund Freud was among the first western authors to write about the unconscious. He believed that so much of what we think and feel, and so much of our personality, wasn't actually available to our conscious minds at any one time. He thought that in order to understand ourselves, we had to be willing to dig deeper into the kind of stuff we don't think about on a daily basis. This is why Freud liked to analyse his patients' dreams. His idea was that when we dream, our unconscious minds are free to express our deeply-held thoughts, desires and feelings.

In short, the unconscious is responsible for generating a lot of our emotions that bubble up to the surface of our conscious minds. Think of your mind as being like a large iceberg in the ocean. The tip of the iceberg, the part that can be seen above water, is your conscious mind. Your unconscious mind, however, is all the stuff that is hidden beneath the water. You might not be aware of it, but your unconscious mind is busy at work all the time, assessing the world around you and shaping the way you feel in response to particular events. Luckily, there are a range of tools and techniques you can use to help you manage your unconscious mind and start reacting to the world in a healthier way. These include meditation and affirmations, and we'll come back to these later in the book.

To become emotionally intelligent, you need to make friends with your unconscious mind. Your conscious, rational mind – the part of you that you use throughout the day when handling various tasks - doesn't always know best. Our conscious minds are typically tugged in many different directions at once, especially if you are busy and trying to multitask. Your unconscious, on the other hand, is free to make deeper and more meaningful judgements. In some cases, it can even save your life.

For example, have you ever been in a situation that your rational, conscious mind judged to be perfectly fine, and yet you still felt uneasy? Have you ever turned down a date, special offer or even a job because someone involved just gave you a 'bad vibe'? This is your unconscious mind helping you out. It is continually monitoring your surroundings below the level of conscious awareness. You should respect its wisdom. If you think back to those times where you listened to your gut instinct, you are probably glad you took those cues from your subconscious.

Why is all this important to remember? Basically, because your emotional intelligence comes from your unconscious mind. Your unconscious mind is the sum total of all your thoughts, feelings and personality traits. Your unconscious mind is on your side at all times, driven by the basic survival instincts that have been passed down over the generations.

Have you ever done something that you thought was 'out of character' or unlike the 'real you'? If you frequently find yourself surprised by your own behaviours, you need to work on your emotional intelligence and take a look at what could be going on beneath the surface of your conscious mind. For example, suppose that you find yourself reaching a decision one Monday that you are utterly sick of your job, draft your letter of resignation, and start ringing employment agencies.

Even if you surprise yourself with the strength of your own emotions and sudden resolve, it probably wasn't so sudden after all. You were probably squashing down weeks, months or even years of irritation triggered by your job. To your unconscious mind, it wouldn't come as a surprise at all! Emotionally intelligent people understand that we don't always understand our own actions a lot of the time, and they aren't scared to admit it either. People with high EQs respect the way in which the conscious and unconscious minds work together. Even when they end up doing something 'out of character,' they trust that there is a reason for their behaviour, and even if the final result is less than perfect, they resolve to learn from it.

If you are in a leadership position, it's especially important to remember that an individual's behaviour may appear to be 'odd' or 'out of character' at times, but in fact make perfect sense in light of their previous experiences and the contents of their unconscious minds. If a member of your team acts in a way that takes you by surprise, exercise your emotional intelligence and avoid overreacting. Instead, trust that there are reasons for your subordinate's behaviour, even if you don't happen to know them. Be open to the idea that the person in question may not fully understand their own actions either, and take a careful, sympathetic approach. Even when you believe that you know a person well, they still have the power to surprise you. A good leader understands that every person is a multi-faceted individual with the power to change and shock those around them. It is important to communicate this value by treating everyone with respect and holding honest, open conversations when difficult situations arise.

Exercise – Alternative Explanations

Get into the habit of adopting an open-minded approach to anticipating and understand the behaviour of other people. Every day, play the 'Other Explanation' game. Whenever a friend, relative or colleague does something that goes against your expectations, try and come up with at least three different explanations for their actions or attitudes. For example, if the receptionist at your place of work doesn't greet you cheerfully as usual when you go into work, you might come up with the following three reasons: That they are preoccupied with a family issue; that they didn't see you when you came in; that they don't feel well. This exercise is especially valuable if you tend to see the worst possible motives and outcomes in the actions of other people. So if you are the sort of person who might perceive a receptionist's change in demeanour as a personal slight, this exercise will remind you to look beyond yourself and consider that other people lead complicated lives that do not revolve around you!

The unconscious mind doesn't just deal in emotions. Lurking within is a set of beliefs about yourself and the world, which in turn influence how you react to various situations. Part of developing your EQ is understanding the link between your pre-existing beliefs and your emotions. This helps you make sense of your own actions, and also makes it possible to discard or re-configure any beliefs that aren't working for you.

For example, let's say that you want to go back to school to retrain for a new career. You have the time, the money, and the grades needed to get onto the course of your choice. Yet at the same time, you feel as though you are holding yourself back. For no good reason, you can't seem to get around to filling in the application form.

What could be going on here? Well, you might have to look beyond your conscious mind and think about what sort of underlying beliefs might be holding you back. Perhaps your parents, friends or an ex-partner think that going back to college as an adult is silly or a waste of time, and you have internalized that belief. Developing your EQ will equip you with the ability to really examine your core beliefs and challenge them. This means you can make choices that are in line with your values, rather than those of other people.

A similar mechanism is at work with memories. For example, you might find that you feel faintly annoyed whenever you are around a particular neighbour or co-worker. Thinking with your logical mind, you can't understand why this is – after all, she hasn't done anything wrong. But look deeper – could there be a less obvious explanation? It may be that this woman reminds you of a friend of your parents,' who scared you as a child. Without you realising it, this early experience could have left an impression on you that means you experience a particular emotional response years later. See what interesting and helpful insights you can come up with when you are willing to examine your previous experiences and beliefs?

Not only is an understanding of the conscious and unconscious minds useful for your own personal development, but it helps you understand the behaviours and motivations of other people. When you accept that other people don't always have perfect control over their feelings – they might be driven by previous memories, for example, that may not even be conscious of – you start to become more compassionate towards them. This helps you adopt a more patient, generous attitude towards others, and in turn this enriches your relationships.

Exercise – Free Association

Sigmund Freud used his theories of the unconscious and conscious mind to formulate his own brand of treatment, psychoanalysis, also known as 'the talking cure.' Basically, he believed that people suffered from mental and emotional distress when they struggled with inner conflicts and desires that they didn't or couldn't face. He believed that the job of a psychotherapist was to probe a patient's unconscious mind and tap into their deepest thoughts. One technique he used to do this was 'free association,' in which he would present a patient with words or phrases and ask them to respond with whatever came into their minds.

This technique is not practiced by many therapists today, but it can still be a useful and entertaining tool if you want to explore what is going on beneath the surface of your conscious mind! Ask a friend to read you a list of random words – these could include feelings, names of objects, or peoples' names – and simply state whatever comes into your head. This can give you a surprisingly rapid insight into the emotions, memories and ideas lurking within your subconscious mind. If nothing else, it can be funny to see the random associations your brain turns up!

What If You Are Continually Surprised By Your Own Actions?

As mentioned above, many of us occasionally act in unusual or unexpected ways, and struggle to make sense of our actions. The more emotionally intelligent you are, the more you will come to accept and even celebrate this part of your nature. However, if you are confused or even disturbed by your own actions, it may be time to seek outside help.

'Help' in this context will probably mean seeing a psychotherapist. It has become increasingly common over the past few couple of decades for people who are undergoing difficulties in life to seek therapy. It is absolutely nothing of which to be ashamed. In fact, the opposite is true! Being able to take responsibility for your personal development is a sign of emotional maturity and development. A good therapist will be able to grant you some insight into even your most baffling and self-defeating behaviours and as a result help you grow your emotional intelligence. Ask your family doctor, close friends, relatives or even HR department at your place of work if you need recommendations. If the first therapist you see doesn't feel like a good fit, find another. It is well worth finding someone you like, because research shows that the most important factor in whether psychotherapy will be successful is the strength of the relationship between therapist and client.

If you are in a leadership position, please remember that in all probability you will have within your team at least one person who has battled psychological or emotional problems at some stage. Recognising that you face your own struggles and being willing to undergo treatment will help you understand such experiences and provide you with the ability to empathise with others in this position if they ever open up to you about such matters.

Emotions, Joy And Fulfilment

In the previous chapter, we looked at why it's unwise to rely on our rational thinking capacities all the time. There is another reason why it's important to develop emotional intelligence: because emotions are a large part of what makes life worth living! Imagine if we were all robot-like beings who only made 'sensible,' 'reasonable' decisions using our conscious minds. How dull would that be? Not only does neglecting your leisure time diminish your own joy in life, but focussing only on work and other 'heavy' responsibilities will make you unattractive and unapproachable to almost everyone else, with the exception of fellow workaholics! If you want to be perceived positively as a leader, it is vital that you appear to be human, just like those you lead. Luckily, this is easily accomplished as long as you put consistent effort into leading a balanced life.

No-one gets to enjoy a perfect life, but most of us at least get to experience feelings of joy, love and peace at some time or another. Many people would say that pleasurable emotional experiences form the bedrock of their fondest memories. For example, think back to your own favourite memory. What makes it stand out for you? Chances are, your best memories have a significant emotional component to them. Thinking about the first time you fell in love might evoke warm feelings of nostalgia. Memories of your college graduation may bring up feelings of pride. Reminiscing about a great holiday with family or friends probably makes you feel happy and grateful. Emotions offer really good value! You get to enjoy the feelings in the moment, but you can also draw upon your stores of positive memories in later years. They can keep you going when things get tough.

Why not go one step further and make a memory scrapbook or keep a few photos pinned somewhere that will make you smile every time you pass it? If you've been meaning to frame some meaningful prints, get it sorted this weekend! In the workplace, you could keep positive images of your team in a prominent position. Little touches like this help everyone feel a sense of solidarity with colleagues, and this can help during times of great pressure. Make sure somebody takes dignified yet light-hearted photos of team-bonding events or socials. A cohesive team will feel closer and are likely to perform better.

Emotionally intelligent people instinctively know that good memories are powerful and can fuel you through dark times. These people know how to make the best use of their feelings, both past and present. As well as understanding the importance of enjoying the moment, they also use positive memories to get them through hard times and build resilience in the face of difficulties.

Emotions also help us in attaining our goals. When you set goals, of course you need to use your rational, conscious mind to choose realistic, suitable targets. However, what actually gets you from start to finish? That's right – emotions! You could choose a goal for purely practical reasons, but think about what happens when you go after a goal you really want, that means a lot to you. You are more likely to achieve it, and as a bonus you are more likely to have a good time along the way.

Another vital aspect of an enjoyable life is humour and laughter. When it comes to making a successful joke, logic alone doesn't cut it. The best jokes and funny stories work because they get an emotional response from those who hear it. You could argue that successful comedians are probably high in emotional intelligence, as they know how to make other people feel happy and relaxed. Other forms of entertainment such as novels, films and videogames rely on the same principle to be effective: they change the way you feel, and in doing so let you escape from day-to-day worries and concerns.

If you are in a position of responsibility at work, it can be tempting to focus on meeting targets and maximising productivity. You may feel compelled to ask your team members to quieten down and focus if they seem to be having a bit too much fun. This is understandable – after all, if everyone veers off task and the company's objectives are not met, you will be held responsible by your line manager and will suffer the consequences. However, a few minutes spent laughing and joking around in the workplace can actually offer a good return on the time invested! This is because laughter is a great way to bond with others, and allows your team to build positive relationships grounded in shared experiences and in-jokes. To be a successful, likeable leader, you need to allow your team the chance to mess around every once in a while. They may not get any work done for a few minutes, but in the long run they will enjoy working under your supervision and be more willing to give you their best effort.

You should now be convinced that we have emotions for a good reason, and that if we are going to get the best from our lives, we need to understand how best to use them. Turn the page and start learning exactly how you can apply the right tools to improve your EQ.

Chapter III:

How To Improve Your Emotional Intelligence

So now that you know the benefits of boosting your EQ, the next question is this: How, exactly, are you are going to achieve this goal? In this chapter, we'll look at three main tools: Meditation, the Emotional Freedom Technique (EFT), and Affirmations. Use all three on a regular basis and you can rapidly improve your EQ.

Why Use These Tools?

These tools have been tried and tested by millions of people before you. Meditation has been practiced as a spiritual and non-spiritual discipline throughout the ages. EFT is a relatively new practice, but has already been embraced by people around the world and is even available as a treatment on the public health service in Britain. Finally, affirmations are a self-help classic for a reason – they work.

In short, these techniques provide you with reliable ways to get in touch with your emotions, control your reactions in difficult situations, and to improve your relationships with others. They will improve your general outlook on the world, make it easier for you to access positive mental states and in turn improve in every area of your life.

Tool Number 1: Meditation

To be emotionally intelligent, you need to learn how to manage your emotions. The first step is to develop the kind of mind-set that will allow you to recognise how you feel, detach yourself from your most intense emotions, and respond appropriately to the situation. In other words, you must learn how to be mindful, and one of the best ways to do that is through regular meditation practice.

Don't worry if the word 'meditation' conjures up images of religious people sitting in uncomfortable positions. You don't need to have any particular beliefs to benefit from meditation as a practice. You simply need some patience and a willingness to learn.

Try the following meditation exercises as a start. See which you like the best. There is no one single best way to meditate – it's about finding what works for you, and then doing it regularly. A sensible goal when you are starting out is to meditate for five minutes each day. As the days and weeks go by, you will notice the positive side-effects in your everyday life. You will become calmer, less disturbed by your emotions, and better able to take a detached, objective view of life events.

Meditation Exercise 1: Focused Attention

Sit on the floor or in a comfortable chair in a quiet room free from distractions. Choose something pleasant or neutral to focus on – this could be a lit candle, a particular spot on the wall, or just your own breathing.

Your task isn't easy, but the instructions are straightforward. For just five minutes, try your best to focus solely on this one thing. In the beginning, you will find this very difficult. You will find that your mind keeps wandering off in many random directions. Don't judge yourself for this. Just try and bring your attention back as soon as possible. Over time, you will find it easier to stay focused for longer. It doesn't matter if you find yourself 'failing.' The important thing is that you keep trying, because as long as you stick with it, you will improve.

Extra Tip: If you find it hard to concentrate or keep your mind clear whilst meditating, give yourself a few minutes at the beginning in which to write down on a piece of paper anything that is bothering you. This will have a reassuring effect, since you know that your worries haven't been forgotten and that you can come back to them later!

Meditation Exercise 2: Walking Meditation

Some people find sitting still for five minutes impossible. If this describes you, or you just feel like experimenting with a different sort of meditation, try a walking-based practice. This also has the added advantage of sun exposure, which is a free and effective way to improve your mood. The endorphins that start flowing when you engage in any kind of activity will also give you a happiness boost!

Find some comfortable footwear and visit a quiet natural environment alone. Woodland or a park in the middle of a weekday afternoon are two good options. Walk at a moderate pace. As you do so, focus on the sensation of moving. Usually when we walk around, we are focusing on something else – perhaps on a conversation we're having, or a job we have to do later in the day, or even just the birds on the lake. In walking meditation, however, your mission is to keep your attention on the feel of the ground beneath your feet, how your muscles feel when they contract and relax, the depth of your breathing, and so on.

Meditation Exercise 3: Loving – Kindness Meditation

This is a variation of the first exercise, but has the additional benefit in that it trains you to feel more compassion towards others. As in the first exercise, you will need to sit in a comfortable position and focus your attention. The difference this time is that you will be focusing on sending loving thoughts and feelings to others.

The easiest way to begin with this kind of practice is to direct your affectionate feelings towards someone you like. As you breathe deeply in and out with your eyes closed, visualize sending them waves of warm light. Think about how much you love them. Focus on how good it feels to dwell on positive feelings. Notice that you can summon these feelings at any time.

If you want a real challenge – and you seriously want to work on your emotional intelligence – try this exercise whilst focusing on someone you don't know well, or even someone you hate. If you can manage to send sincere wishes of goodwill to people who rub you up the wrong way, you are well on your way to being an emotionally intelligent person with a positive, compassionate attitude towards those around you. Others will pick up on this attitude and your relationships will improve.

Going The Extra Step: Consider Going On A Retreat

If you find yourself becoming very interested in meditation, you may consider going on a meditative retreat, which is often conducted at least partially in silence. Typically, a retreat will be conducted in a simple, calm environment in a rural setting. Those attending will usually have to attend classes in meditation every day, and undertake communal duties such as cooking and cleaning with others. Accommodation is often simple and decorated in such a way to minimise distractions and reminders of everyday life. This kind of activity can be scary, but in the quiet or silent setting you are forced to come face to face with your own thoughts and feelings. For those early in their journey to greater emotional intelligence, this may be too intense an exercise.

Tool Number 2: Emotional Freedom Technique (EFT)

Learn EFT and you'll be able to put yourself in a calm state of mind whenever you feel like it. The ability to retain your composure even when your emotions are running high is an important part of emotional intelligence, and EFT can help you do just that.

All you have to do is lightly tap on various points around the body. This theory borrows from Chinese acupuncturists, who believe that many health and emotional problems are the result of energy flowing incorrectly around the body. The idea is that by tapping on certain areas such as the back of your hands, you can safely and quickly release negative emotions.

Here is an example of an EFT exercise. Try it the next time you are feeling stressed or overwhelmed. Some practitioners will use affirmations or special eye movements, but you can try this exercise as a good starting point.

EFT Exercise

Take off your glasses, watch and any other jewellery. According to some people, these can block energy flow in the body, so are best removed before you begin.

Notice how your body feels. Notice the negative emotions you are facing. Put a label on them, and acknowledge them. Choose one particular feeling you want to eliminate. For instance, if you are feeling generally unhappy or frustrated at work you could focus on your anger whilst tapping for a while, then repeat the exercise whilst focusing on feelings of frustration. Rate how strong this emotion currently is, on a scale of 1-10.

Now comes the fun part! Whilst focusing on your chosen emotion, tap on any of the following body parts lightly with the first two fingers of either hand. It doesn't matter which side of the body you tap. Just keep tapping at a steady pace for a couple of minutes, until the feelings begin to subside. You could even do this discreetly in a tense, public situation like an important business meeting.

Some tapping points to try:

- Outer edge of your hand, just beneath the little finger
- Chin crease, just beneath your lower lip
- Approximately one inch below either eye
- Four inches below your armpit, on your rib cage

Finally, rate the strength of your emotion again. It should have subsided significantly. If it hasn't, don't worry – just tap for another couple of minutes.

Tool Number 3: Affirmations

Put simply, affirmations are statements that you repeat either aloud or in your head on a regular basis. As you say these affirmations, they gradually work on your unconscious mind. As a result, you will see your behaviours begin to change. A good affirmation is positive, short, and memorable. It is also in the present tense, and keeps you mindful of your current situation.

If you want to use affirmations to help you build your EQ, you could try some of these:

I am becoming more emotionally intelligent.
I am in touch with my emotions.
I have great relationships with others.
Whatever the feeling, I can handle it.
I have a high EQ.

Some people like to say their affirmations when they first wake up in the morning, whereas others like to repeat them just before going to sleep as a way of ending the day on a positive note. Experiment and see what works best for you.

Affirmations work by replacing negative thoughts such as 'I'm no good with people' or 'I have no confidence' with more positive thoughts such as 'I have good people skills' and 'I am confident.' When you think about it, it's obvious that our emotions are shaped by our thoughts, so why not try your best to think something more uplifting?

If you feel too self-conscious – even when alone – to say your affirmations aloud, why not write them down instead? You can do this discreetly in a journal, or if you have sufficient privacy, write them on pieces of paper and stick them somewhere obvious, such as on your bathroom mirror. Alternatively, make an affirmation part of the wallpaper on your phone, tablet or computer.

How To Banish Unhelpful Negative Thoughts With Aversion Therapy

As you work on instilling more helpful ways of thinking, you will start to realize just how much your existing negative thoughts are holding you back. It can be quite alarming, when you start paying attention, to find that you have been telling yourself how useless/disorganized/hopeless you are. This is the flipside of using positive affirmations – casting aside your old, outdated thoughts. This is necessary for developing a positive self of self, awareness, and emotional intelligence.

A classic technique used in various forms of therapy is aversion training. To do this, simply find a regular rubber band and slip it around your wrist. When you notice yourself engaging in unhelpful, repetitive thoughts, ping the band against your wrist. The aim isn't to hurt yourself or to leave a mark. Your goal is just to jolt your awareness back to the present moment and away from toxic thoughts that don't serve you in any way. Remember, learning how to recognise and discard such thought patterns is key in developing emotional intelligence.

As a leader, this exercise will also help you better identify with any members of your team who may suffer from low self-confidence. Everyone experiences periods of time in which they doubt their own abilities and ruminates on what has gone wrong in the past. If you are willing to put in the work required to understand your own tendencies to put yourself down, this will make you more sympathetic to others' struggles. In turn, they will pick up on your empathy and are more likely to come to you for help and support. When team members start to do this, you can take this as a sign that you have built real trust and rapport with others.

How To Build New Habits

Habits are not built overnight. It takes time to learn new skills, and raising your EQ is no different. As a general rule, it takes 21-30 days to implement a new habit, so be patient. It's also common to require a few attempts to establish new patterns of behaviour, so don't beat yourself up if new habits fail to 'stick' the first couple of times. Set aside some time each day to practice each of the above exercises. Choosing the same time every day will help you settle into a routine, which will in turn solidify your new habits. Although it may be difficult to meditate for more than a few minutes at a time when you begin, aim to use the above tools for approximately 20 minutes per day. You can fit them around your existing schedule, for example by using tapping during a work break or fitting in some meditation whilst waiting for your bus to arrive. This way, they will become part of your regular routine and exert a significant positive impact on your life.

If you know someone else who is interested in self-development, why not suggest to them that you become accountability partners? If you are both trying to make positive changes in your lives, set up an arrangement whereby you check in with one another on a weekly or even daily basis. Every time you talk, be honest with one another about the progress you are making on your self-development goals. When you succeed, congratulate one another. When you fail – and there's no shame in taking a few attempts when making big changes – gently but firmly challenge one another to do better.

By the way, building this kind of relationship gives you a chance to develop your relationship skills even further. Undertaking a challenge with someone else gives you the chance to empathise with another person who is facing the same struggles as you. Remember – empathy, patience and being able to listen to someone else are core components of emotional intelligence, so seize any chance you have to grow your skills in this area.

If you are a leader, you might be wondering how you could introduce these activities to your team in such a way that they would benefit from them too. You have a number of options, and the right one to pick will depend on your seniority, workplace culture, and the personalities of your team members. For example, a conservative team probably won't be receptive to the notion of communal meditation first thing in the morning, but they may be open to a lunchtime lecture on the benefits of positive psychology and the use of affirmations. You could take an even more subtle approach and leave a range of relevant books in the staffroom for everyone to read at break times.

A Word On Multi-tasking

When you have many things to do, it can be tempting to try and tackle more than one at a time, i.e. to multi-task. On the face of it, multi-tasking seems like a great idea and when you first read the suggestions above you may have considered combining them, perhaps by using affirmations during your meditation practice. However, multi-tasking is not actually the best approach if you want to be productive. Juggling multiple tasks at the same time leads to stress and even burnout if done over a long period of time.

Instead, aim to live a life of focus. Rather than attempting to get everything done at once, set yourself realistic targets and to-do lists. Work through each item on your list one at a time, maintaining your attention on the task at hand. If you begin a regular meditation practice, you will naturally find that even when you have lots of work to do, you will be better-equipped to calmly get your work done without falling into the trap of panicking.

Bonus Tip 1: Become A Body Language Expert

If you want to detect and react appropriately to other peoples' emotions, you need to be able to pick up on what they're feeling from their body language. Most of us have at least a decent grasp of the basics. For example, you generally know that if someone is happy, they will smile, and if they are very sad or scared, they will cry. However, to be truly emotionally intelligent you must become a body language master.

Here are a few body language tips to start you off:

Consider the person's posture: In the animal kingdom, dominant animals take up more space than subordinates. They feel entitled to the extra legroom and have no problem asserting their status. It's the same in humans. One of the quickest ways of judging who holds the most power in any situation is to note who is claiming the biggest portion of the table, the largest chair, and who feels most at ease spreading their arms and legs. The more space someone takes up, the more secure they are in their own power. By contrast, subordinates and those lacking in confidence will try and take up the least space possible. If you are in a leadership role, communicate self-esteem and self-belief by standing with your feet shoulder-width apart, opening your shoulders, and making sure your legs are not crossed when sitting down.

Consider the direction in which their feet are pointing: As a general rule, the direction in which a person is pointing their feet indicates where they would like to be or what they would like to be doing. If you are in a meeting and another party has their feet angled towards the door, this is a sign that you need to work harder to engage them.

Consider whether there is any mirroring going on: The next time you have the chance to observe two friends or romantic partners, watch for body language mirroring. When two people have a strong emotional or psychological rapport, they will tend to copy one another's body language. You can use this to your advantage by subtly mirroring someone in conversation. For example, if they put their hands on the table, wait a few seconds and then slowly do the same. This builds emotional intimacy, and makes them more likely to pay attention to what you have to say.

Consider the angle of their head: Confident people who are secure in their positions and convictions tend to look straight ahead, making regular eye contact. Whilst a lack of eye contact isn't necessarily suspicious – it could just mean that a person is shy – it does not inspire confidence. Shy people tend to tilt their heads to one side, which is a sign of submission and low self-esteem. If you are in a leadership position, aim to hold your head up straight and make appropriate eye contact (no staring!) at whoever it is you are talking to. This will communicate trustworthiness and self-respect.

Consider how they are positioning their hands: Someone who is confident and feels safe will typically move their hands only to make an occasional gesture. However, someone who is anxious or angry will twist their hands together, clench their fists, or pull on accessories or items of clothing. If you want to be seen as a credible leader, keep your hands still unless you need to gesture to make an important point. Resist the urge to touch your face, even if it itches, as this will undermine your credibility.

Don't jump to conclusions based on a single cue or incident: Although body language knowledge is useful, take care not to draw quick judgements based on a single cue. For instance, someone itching the back of their neck could be nervous about an impending business deal – or they could just have forgotten to take the label out of their new shirt! Take patterns of behaviour into account and don't worry too much about an isolated cue.

There are many decent books out there on this topic, but the best strategy in learning how to read body language is to practice. Whenever possible, take note of what messages others are sending with their bodies. Are they in a 'closed' position, in which their limbs are held near the body? Then they may be feeling shy, anxious, or hiding something from you. Perhaps they are more 'open,' with their arms and legs apart? If this is the case, they probably feel more relaxed and at ease. Become an expert people watcher. Where possible, find out whether your guesses were correct. Observe someone, take a reading of their emotional state, and then ask them how they are. Of course they won't always tell you the truth, but it can be rewarding to hear that your guess was correct!

Bonus Tip 2: Choose To Change Your Mental State With The Facial Feedback Hypothesis

Wouldn't it be great if you could choose to feel better whenever you wanted to? Well, you can – at least, to some extent. The following technique is based in research findings looking at something called the Facial Feedback Hypothesis. Carry out both parts to gain a full appreciation of how it works. The contrast will amaze you!

Part 1

1. Sit down on a chair. Drop your shoulders, clasp your hands together tightly and stare down at the floor. If you prefer to stand, lean against the wall in such a way that you feel physically uncomfortable, and look at the ground.
2. Frown hard, using as many muscles around your eyes and forehead as possible.
3. Remain in this position for at least a minute.
4. Notice how you feel. Even if you felt quite upbeat when you started, you'll probably find that you feel dejected, anxious, and negative.

Part 2

Now induce a very different state within yourself:

1. Sit up straight in your chair, or if you prefer to stand, check that your posture is as upright as possible.
2. Put on a 'happy face.' Smile broadly, and try to relax the muscles in your jaw, neck and shoulders. If it helps, imagine that you have just received a piece of really good news, or seen something that usually makes you feel better. This could be a favourite person or even a piece of art you like.
3. Stay in this position for at least a minute.
4. Notice the results – do you feel happier?

According to research carried out by psychologists, this exercise should lift your mood. Studies have shown that when people are forced to assume a smiling facial expression, they rate cartoons as more amusing than when they are forced to adopt a neutral expression. Why? Because it turns out that the link between body language and emotions goes both ways. We all know that when we are happy, we tend to laugh and smile. However, research has shown that if we arrange our faces and bodies so that they take on the appearance of happiness, this sends a message to our brains that we are happy. As a result, our mood lifts. Try it and see!

Some people don't appreciate the value of deliberately cultivating positivity, and so may be sceptical of people like you who understand why it is so important to carry yourself in a positive way, even if things aren't going quite as well as you'd like. If you lead a team, share this exercise with others and they'll understand why you are trying so hard to convey a positive attitude. You can't exactly give out posture awards, but you can certainly model positive body language for other people. In turn, their mood will improve and there is a good chance that their general job and life satisfaction will improve. This will lead to a boost in team morale and will establish your reputation as an inspirational leader who spurs on their team to positive action.

Advanced Exercise For Improving Your EI: Practice and Feedback Via Role Play

Much of what you learn about your own emotions and those of other people will be gained through everyday life experience. However, there is one technique you can employ that will allow you to practice before or after you come up against particular situations in real life – role play. This isn't for those who are easily embarrassed or inhibited, but it can be tremendously effective. In the first chapter, you read about some research carried out with students who were taught how to improve their EI over the course of a few weeks. One technique used in that intervention was role play, in which students were asked to act out various scenarios in which they demonstrated emotionally intelligent and emotionally unintelligent behaviour.

You can try this with a trusted friend or colleague. First, think of a situation in which you often struggle to know how to handle your emotions, keep your mood level, or react in an appropriate way to another person. Describe it to your friend, and ask them to help you rehearse a brand new way of behaving. Don't worry if your acting skills aren't perfect! As long as you aim to reproduce the scenario as faithfully as possible and experiment with new ways of behaving, you will have achieved your aim.

For example, let's say that last week, you had to invite one of your team into the office for a meeting. Let's say that this meeting was tough because you had to inform this person that their performance was not up to standard and that for the next few weeks they would be supervised more closely and an action plan implemented to improve their success rate. Imagine that this meeting was difficult because the person in question does not respond well to criticism, and is also under increased stress at home following the birth of a new baby.

In such a situation, you could tell your friend how you handled the meeting, and demonstrate during the role play how you used your voice, body language and choice of words to communicate with this person. Once you have acted out the key moments, ask your friend for some honest feedback. How do they think you are coming across? Be prepared for some harsh feedback. Sometimes we think that we are acting in a sensitive, emotionally intelligent way only to later learn that another person experienced us as cold or insensitive. However, although this feedback can be hard to hear, it is invaluable if you are going to seriously boost your EI. Don't forget to thank your friend for their input and of course to return the favour.

This can also work well prior to an emotionally demanding situation. If you know, for example, that you have to let someone know that they are being made redundant over the next few days, it is a good idea to mentally rehearse how you are going to handle the situation prior to actually doing the deed. It is an even better idea, if you are nervous, to practice saying the key words to someone else within a role play context. This allows you to practice not only forming suitably sensitive words and phrases, but also to prepare yourself for the difficult emotions you may feel such as guilt or anxiety. In this particular example whereby you must make someone redundant, knowing in advance that you are likely to feel very anxious is helpful information as you could then remind yourself to take several deep breaths before and during the meeting in order to keep your body as relaxed as possible.

Undertaking role play like this is also a means in itself of improving emotional intelligence. It requires you to be open, honest and vulnerable about how you feel and to act them out. It requires that you maintain an open mind and listen to what your role play partner has to say. Finally, you will need to get into the habit of offering constructive responses to your partner. Be honest, but not unnecessarily brutal. For example, offer positive feedback before giving suggestions for improvement, and remind them how brave they are for agreeing to do this exercise with you in the first place. It takes a lot of emotional maturity and can be scary, but ultimately you will both gain insight into your emotional patterns.

Chapter IV:

How To Use Emotional Intelligence
In Specific Situations

How To Use Your Emotions As A Guide When Making Decisions

We've already taken a look at the power of your unconscious mind, and how you can make smart decisions by paying attention to your emotions. But how, exactly, should you do that? In this chapter you will learn lots of tips and tricks to get in touch with your feelings and use what you find in making the best possible decision, whatever your situation.

Try some of the techniques below. If the first one you try doesn't feel right, move onto another. They may feel unnatural at first, but keep on trying. Emotional intelligence is such a valuable resource that it's worth taking the time and effort to develop it to the best of your ability.

You can use these techniques when facing a tricky situation at either work or home. The principles are the same. Whether you want to be a better leader at work or a more attentive spouse, monitoring your emotions and using them wisely when making decisions will help.

Allow yourself a minute to sit still and be quiet
Try one of the meditation exercises mentioned in the previous chapter. Once you've finished, follow it up with a short period spent in silence. Ask yourself a simple question – 'What do I really

feel about this situation?' Sometimes, our emotions need to be given space to come out and breathe if we are going to have the chance to make the most of them. You might even get a single thought or revelation. For example, you might be sitting there wondering whether to sell your home and and move to the coast, and suddenly become aware that yes, you have always wanted to live near the sea and that this decision is the right one for you. You may even get a mental image along with a particular feeling. Pay attention to what these images are trying to tell you.

If you don't have your own office at work, it's worth taking the time to find an empty room or even, in desperate moments, a quiet cupboard! If you are a manager, make sure you respect the needs of your subordinates to take their time over making decisions too. Obviously you need to ensure that your team meets deadlines, but don't expect people to make important decisions until significant time pressure and get them right every time. Extend the same courtesy to your boss as well – remember that they have many pressing obligations and demands on their time. A good leader works well with those above and below them on the organizational ladder.

Grab a paper and pen and brainstorm what you feel
Give yourself as long as you need to write down absolutely anything that comes to mind, even if it seems silly. Do this in private if you feel as though others would judge you for doing it. Now look over what you have written. Sometimes we enjoy renewed clarity when a situation is set down on a page in black and white! You may not even realise you feel a certain way until you give yourself permission to note it down. If you are leading a team, try this activity as a group brainstorming session. Make it clear that everyone is expected to contribute, and that passing negative judgements on other peoples' ideas will not be tolerated. Join in and contribute your own ideas – if you want other people to respect you, then never ask them to do what you refuse to do yourself.

Tune in and listen to your body

Your body is only too willing to give you a few clues, if you give it a chance and listen carefully. If you find that you get aches, pains or other symptoms on a regular basis, your body could be trying to tell you that something isn't right.

For example, if you start paying attention to those strange tension headaches that you get every time you visit your parents, you may realise that visiting your family is causing you more worry than you might have wanted to admit. You could then use this information when making decisions such as whether to go on a vacation with them, or move closer, or invite them to stay with you during the holidays.

Try the daily emotional temperature technique

If you are having trouble making a large decision, try taking your emotional temperature over a period of a few days or even weeks. For example, say you are having trouble deciding whether or not to leave your job, or end a relationship. Pick a time of day, perhaps when you get in from work, and then take a few minutes to note down how you feel about your decision.

This is useful because sometimes we find it hard to remember how we truly felt about something at the time, even if the time in question was just a few days ago. Taking a regular reading allows you to step back and take a long-ranging view of your true feelings about a particular issue, and this information can be helpful in making a good choice. To continue the example above, you might decide to write a few words about how you are feeling about your job when you come home and do this for a period of one month. At the end of this month, if you find page after page is filled with statements about how terrible your job is, you can safely say that your emotion – hatred towards your work – is consistent, and that your job is just a long succession of bad days. You can make a decision to resign and look for something else, knowing that you aren't acting on impulse.

However, you might find that there are fewer days on which you think 'this is awful' than you might expect. This raises a different question: what is it about those bad days that leaves you feeling like you want to quit? Perhaps you can spot a pattern. For instance, do you tend to feel bad or angry every Wednesday afternoon just after the weekly team meeting? Once you've identified patterns, you can decide whether there is any way of changing or eliminating anything that triggers certain emotions in you. For example, could you pinpoint what it is about the weekly meeting that makes you so annoyed and suggest to your boss that you do things differently? If there's nothing you can do, of course, then you may feel it's time to move on. If certain people in your team trigger certain emotions in you, this technique can help you see patterns where previously there was only chaos.

Talk to friends or family you can trust about their experiences
You will probably find that if you ask those close to you about a time they based a decision on a powerful emotion, they will tell you that they made a wise choice. Sometimes it makes 'logical sense' to pursue a particular path, yet our hearts and emotional selves say otherwise. This is especially the case when it comes to making decisions about romantic relationships, where a little bit of instinct goes a long way.

Not only will you be able to learn from other peoples' experiences if you do this, but you will also improve your relationships with family members and friends. This is because when you listen to someone's story and take a real interest in what they are saying, you can better understand how they got to be the person they are today. As a result, you gain increased insight and empathy for them, which is likely to result in greater feelings of love, compassion and closeness. Being able to open up to others and listen with attention is an important component of emotional intelligence.

Why You Should Make An Effort To Enjoy Yourself

When we feel happy, we are more at ease with ourselves and the world around us. This means that we are more receptive to positive feelings towards others, which increases the likelihood of forming successful relationships.

When you actively seek out new experiences, connections and knowledge, you become a more interesting and attractive person. Moreover, you begin to attract people on a similar wavelength – the sort of people who seek out meaningful relationships with others, who take a positive view of the world, and who tend to have high levels of emotional intelligence. When you form friendships with these type of people, you will have more opportunities to learn from others, to form meaningful relationships, and to learn more about the world around you. In time, you will become a more well-rounded person at ease in a variety of social situations, which makes you more likely to succeed in your personal and professional life.

If it's been a while since you deliberately set out to have fun and mix things up, here are a few ideas to get you started:

- Make a list of little things that give you joy, and do at least two every day.
This could be something as simple as a a hot shower with your favourite shower gel, five minutes spent playing with your dog in the garden, or a quick chat on the phone with your best friend.

- Challenge yourself to find three new ways of enjoying yourself over the next month.
Start by looking at the events pages in your local newspaper or online. Perhaps you could try out a new type of music event, or see a play that you normally wouldn't consider watching? Ask a friend to come with you and make some new memories that you can both enjoy for years to come.

- Consider taking up a new hobby or pastime.

Have you always wanted to learn how to work with clay, or speak Italian? Look out for local classes in your area and attend if possible. This has the benefit of giving you the chance to not only learn new skills, but also to meet new people and practice forming new friendships.

- Work on developing the kind of attitude that allows you to find joy in the small moments of everyday life.

When you notice something positive that brings you joy, take a couple of seconds to savour the moment and to feel grateful. If you believe in God, you could even send out a quick prayer of thanks.

- Throw a party and tell everyone to bring along a guest you haven't met before.

You can make several new connections in one evening, and probably have fun along the way.

- Try to enjoy yourself at work, even if you have a tough assignment.

Start with your workspace. Try and change what you can – the décor, the parking, your chair. It's the little things. Plan something nice for each lunchtime, and if all else fails, plan something to look forward to in the evening.

Make it a habit to keep your life interesting, and you will find that your new attitude and empathy for other people will come across clearly at both work and play.

Think Carefully About Your Media Consumption

If you find yourself frequently drawn to stories or websites that make you feel bad, consider a complete media detox for a few days. Ask yourself whether the media you watch or read makes you feel helpless, envious, or generally negative. How much value does it really add to your life?

If you don't feel ready for the detox challenge yet, at least try a monitoring exercise. For one day, carry a piece of paper and a pen around with you and make a note of all the media you consume, together with how it makes you feel. You don't have to write dozens of in-depth diary entries, just a few notes that will make sense when you come to review them later. Your task is to identify how the media you consume throughout an average day impacts upon your mood, and then use this information to make some informed decisions about how you choose which websites, magazines, books and so forth to read in the future.

For example, you might have fallen into the habit of checking celebrity gossip sites during your morning coffee break, yet never stopped to really think about whether it might be affecting you. Now let's say you decided to pay attention one morning and note down how looking at these sites really makes you feel. You may find that actually, although they are entertaining for a few minutes and distract you from work-related problems, they make you feel resentful, envious or judgemental. These are not traits you want to encourage within yourself when developing emotional intelligence.

On the other hand, you might find that reading a news site about current affairs makes you feel well-connected to others in the world, well-read, and intelligent. When you really think about the significant effect of different kinds of media, it seems obvious that you ought to be careful about where you let your eyeballs fall! A quick five-minute sweep of a quality news site should be enough to let you keep up with everything going on in the world without pulling you into a rabbit hole of negative feelings and distractions.

Music and sounds are another consideration. The music we listen to has a direct effect on our moods, and this can have a negative impact on your ability to manage your emotions. For example, if you choose to listen to sad songs on a regular basis, your mood isn't going to be elevated! If however you make a conscious choice to turn on something more upbeat, this will spur you on and keep you motivated even in the face of difficult tasks. Save the slow, melancholy tracks for occasional use only. When you feel down or discouraged, use music therapy to brighten your mood. Put on a track that matches your negative emotion, but then follow it up with something slightly happier. Finally, put on something totally happy and joyful. This will bring you out of your slump gently. Knowing techniques to manage your emotions is an important part of being an emotionally intelligent person. If you are in leadership position, see whether other people at work would mind you putting on some music or ambient noise. Remember that not everyone will be able to concentrate in an environment other than silence, so you will need to respect that everyone will react differently to this suggestion.

Chapter V:

What Happens When
You Increase Your EQ

So what exactly will happen now that you've started improving your EQ? In short: every area of your life should begin to improve.

Clarity At Work

As your own emotional self-awareness grows, you will start to better understand the dynamics among your colleagues. For example, let's say you have to work with two people who are both perfectly nice, yet frequently argue or snipe at one another and make the office atmosphere unpleasant. With your newfound emotional intelligence, you may find it easier to 'read' both these individuals and realise that they both use defensive body language, refuse to listen properly, and engage in other habits commonly seen in low-EQ people. Now you might feel as though the situation is less of a mystery! This kind of understanding is especially valuable if you are responsible for running a team or department and have to maintain harmony in a group.

You may realise that you are working for a low-EQ boss who doesn't know how to respond to the emotions of other people, or who fails to manage their own feelings at work, or both. Luckily, with your new understanding of emotional intelligence, you can spot the signs of a low EQ quickly and adjust your communication accordingly. You can't force anyone to try and develop these skills, but you can adapt your own behaviour. For example, if your boss frequently brings their personal issues into the office and shows an inability to set proper boundaries, you can make a conscious decision not to let the situation escalate. In fact, you can defuse it by keeping your voice calm and your body language positive.

You will also be better able to make decisions at work, both on a small day-to-day level (such as how to delegate the workload on a project) and on a broader scale (such as whether you ought to seek out additional training, ask for a transfer, or even leave your employer for a new line of work altogether).

Clarity In Relationships

So many relationships suffer, or even end, because people struggle to communicate their true feelings and desires to one another. When you raise your EQ, these difficulties begin to melt away. This isn't to say that you will never have relationship problems ever again, but you can significantly improve your chances at a loving, mutually beneficial relationship by increasing your emotional intelligence.

For a start, by learning to understand and appreciate your feelings, you will learn what kind of person you are and therefore what sort of partner would suit you best. This may mean that you come to the realisation that your current significant other isn't quite right for you. This could mean a radical life change. Perhaps you might even conclude that you'd be better off single than with someone who doesn't fully appreciate your own unique traits and personality.

Most relationships contain some degree of conflict and strife. Very few couples get along perfectly all the time. In fact, a total lack of conflict is almost a cause for concern, because it suggests that one or both of you are suppressing your true feelings. Another possibility is that one of you is scared of the other.

Occasional rows are nothing to be afraid of, especially if one or both of you are undergoing major life changes or suffering from chronic stress. As an emotionally intelligent person, you know this. Even better, you have the tools to argue in a constructive fashion. Rather than setting out to 'beat' your partner or prove that you are right and they are wrong, you should consider making understanding your partner's point of view your primary goal. People with high EQs know that it's more important to reach a place of mutual, shared understanding and to feel empathy for the other person rather than give into any urges to get angry and assert dominance. Being emotionally intelligent means taking the long view of a situation. You begin to understand that acting on your first instinct or reaction may not yield the best outcome in the long run.

Productivity

Have you ever tried to sit down and focus on a particular task whilst feeling especially angry, frustrated, sad, or even over-excited? If you don't know how to manage your emotions, you can lose hours or even days of precious time. If you can't identify, label and manage your feelings, you can end up ruminating on them and thinking about nothing else.

When you become skilled at spotting the emotions that rise up within you, you'll never find yourself in this situation again. You will learn to acknowledge your emotions and then react appropriately, rather than sacrificing your productivity. This is not about completely boxing off your emotions from your everyday life, just about putting them in their proper place as useful guides that should nevertheless not overwhelm you completely.

Joy

Even if developing your emotional intelligence had no practical effect on your career or relationships, it would still be worth learning just for the feelings of joy it can bring. When you learn how to handle your emotions and how to encourage feelings of happiness within yourself, you can live each day knowing that whatever happens, you are always capable of summoning positive feelings.

Even If You Don't Notice, Others Will

As you become more in touch with your own feelings, you will naturally want to take an inventory of your progress on a regular basis. However, sometimes you might feel as though you aren't making quite as much headway as you would like. During these times, it might help to remember that even if you aren't where you want to be, other people will be recognising – and benefitting – from the changes you are trying to make.

For example, you might be concerned with your feelings of anger and be trying to recognise it more often in your daily life. Even if you haven't yet mastered the art of pinning down what triggers these feelings, other people will probably realise that you making more of an effort to grow your self-awareness. Give yourself credit for trying, and remember that it takes a few weeks to change old patterns of thinking.

If you are a leader, rest assured that those you are responsible for managing will notice the change in you. They will feel more comfortable opening up to you and come to appreciate you as a real, complex human being just like them.

Conclusion for Emotional Intelligence

Thank you for choosing this book! I want to wish you many congratulations on starting your journey towards a higher EQ. Now that you've finished reading and have tried out some exercises along the way, you should be feeling as though you are better able to recognise and manage your own emotions and those of other people. Every area of your life should start improving rapidly. You might wonder how you managed before learning about emotional intelligence! Remember that maximising your EQ is a lifelong project, so take a long-term view and make a commitment to becoming the best possible version of yourself.

Finally, if you enjoyed this book, please leave a review for it on Amazon. Thank you.

References

Barling, J., Slater, F., & Kelloway, E.K. (2000). Transformational leadership and emotional intelligence: an exploratory study. *Leadership & Organization Development Journal, 21, 3,* 157-161.

Petrides, K.V., & Furnham, A. (2000). Gender Differences in Measured and Self-Estimated Trait Emotional Intelligence. *Sex Roles, 42, 5/6,* 449-461.

Pool, L.D., & Qualter, P. (2012). Improving emotional intelligence and emotional self-efficacy through a teaching intervention for university students. *Learning and Individual Differences, 22,* 306-312.

Yalcin, B.M., Karahan, T.F., Ozcelik, M., & Igde, F.A. (2008). The Effects of an Emotional Intelligence Program on the Quality of Life and Well-Being of Patients With Type 2 Diabetes Mellitus. *The Diabetes Educator, 34, 6,* 1013-1024.

LEADERSHIP

How to make difficult co-workers respect,
admire and follow you

DISCLAIMER

The information in this book is presented for purposes of education and information only. The author is in no way liable for any outcomes sustained by the reader as the direct or indirect result of the implementation of any advice contained herein. If you know or suspect that you require professional help you must consult with a suitably-qualified person.

Contents

You Are A Leader!

Who is this book for?

Congratulations! If you've picked up this book, you have probably earned a leadership or management role. This may represent a promotion for you, and a new challenge that will stretch you professionally and personally. You may be lying awake at night, anxious about what awaits you. You might be wondering whether your colleagues will respect you, whether your team will look up to you as an authority figure, whether others in the workplace will perceive you differently as a result of your new role, whether you can deliver on targets for your line manager...and the list goes on. You have a lot to think about, and you may be starting to panic.

Fear not. This book can help. We're going to look at the most common fears and issues new leaders face, and why it's important to take a pro-active approach to developing your own leadership potential.

Even the most accomplished leaders started where you are now – nervous about this next stage in their professional lives. The way you are feeling now is completely normal, and can be overcome as long as you are willing to put in the time and effort to understand the most common leadership obstacles new leaders face and how they can be solved. You will learn how to win over even awkward colleagues!

Let's start by taking a closer look at some those worries.

1. That you won't be competent; that your knowledge simply won't be sufficient for the role.

No matter how long you have been with a company, you may still feel as though you lack the relevant training for your new role. If you are moving to a new organization to take up a management role for the first time, then you also face the usual anxiety that comes with being a 'new hire.'

2. That people who have showed faith in you will be disappointed.

Being awarded a promotion by a long-term mentor or manager you respect is a terrific compliment, as is earning a glowing reference from a former employer that allows you to move onto a better-paying job with more responsibilities. However, the downside is that you may feel a sense of pressure. What if you underperform and disappoint those who have shown belief in you?

3. That you may lose some friends at work as a result of your promotion.

If you have worked with the same group of people for months or even years, there can be shifts in the interpersonal dynamics should you be promoted. You may now find yourself having to manage people you consider to be friends. This may profoundly affect your social life. You should be prepared for the possibility that if you are remaining with the same company to take up a management position, some people may not be able to perceive you in the same way, and some may even be too envious or intimidated to continue your friendship.

4. That you will spend too much time managing people and not enough time driving the business forward.

A leader is supposed to lead, and managers are supposed to manage. However, it is possible to become too embroiled in petty details at the expense of advancing the company objectives. New managers often worry that they will spend too long in meetings, for example, at the expense of their other duties.

5. That you won't be able to handle difficult co-workers.

This may be the most worrying item on the list! There's a good reason why competent leaders are so well-respected and often well-paid: managing a team and getting the best possible performance from them is hard work for many reasons. At some point in your career as a leader – perhaps even from the first day – you will have to deal with co-workers who are ill-tempered, bossy, awkward, or just plain difficult.

It's quite a list, isn't it? Luckily, this book will tell you how to handle common problems you can expect to face. Implement the ideas you find in here and you can look forward to the following outcomes:

1. Your social skills will develop.

Once you understand what people look for in a leader and try and relate to them accordingly, you will become more comfortable in social situations. This will boost your confidence in your ability to communicate with other people and understand each of your team member's wants, needs and problems.

2. You will be able to extract the best possible performance from your team.

A good leader boosts team morale. Even when things are going badly or the company is facing multiple setbacks, an inspiring leader gets results.

3. You will be able to share your expertise with others.

An accomplished leader brings not only people skills but background knowledge to the role. As you establish yourself as a leader worthy of respect, you will be given many opportunities to impart your industry and practical knowledge to the people you manage and this can be very rewarding. Once you have been successfully leading a team for a while, you'll also be able to share another kind of knowledge – the kind that comes with fruitful management experience. You may have the privilege of mentoring other leaders, and develop rewarding professional relationships.

4. You will be able to have more influence on the company.

Promotion to a management role indicates that you have demonstrated your potential to make a lasting difference to the organization. Multiple stakeholders will be watching you to see what kind of impression you make on the company. Whilst this is nerve-wracking, it's important that you appreciate the opportunity you have been given. Prove yourself as a competent leader and your views will be respected more than ever before. This means that, increasingly, you will be able to influence the organization's direction and profits. In turn, of course, this means that you are more likely to gain further promotion and a higher salary!

Turn the page and learn how to take the first step towards being a great leader: making a positive impression on others.

7 Ways To Win With People

If you are to be a successful manager, you need to learn to make a great positive impression not only on your team, but also customers, your managers, and everyone else with an interest in the success of your organization.

All of the points listed in this chapter are relevant from your very first day in the role. In fact, they may even be relevant before this point, especially if you have the opportunity to meet your new team before your contract formally begins! Hopefully, your new employer will want you to feel as comfortable as possible in your new role. You may be asked to attend a 'meet the team' meeting, or even a series of meetings, in advance of your arrival. If you are offered this chance, take it! It's vital that you meet everyone on your team as soon as possible, and take the opportunity to create a positive first impression.

Creating an excellent first impression and winning people over cannot be reduced to a set of behaviors. It's more about your mindset and how you approach the situation. Think of the following guidelines as a set of principles to follow, not a set recipe for success!

Principle 1: Uphold a set of suitable values.

Think about the kind of leader that you want to be. If you take a moment to review your experience as a team member working under the direction of a more senior member of staff, you will realize that some of your managers will have much more competent and inspirational than others. In all likelihood, the sorts of leaders you have most admired in the past will have been not only competent and knowledgeable in their fields, but people of principle and integrity.

Specifically, you should be looking to model the following values: honesty, transparency, a strong work ethic, focus, compassion, commitment to the organization you serve, and the ability to be open to new ideas. Of course, your company will have their own specific set of values and core ideas, and you should look to uphold these too.

What might this look like in practice? An honest and transparent leader will share all relevant information and news with their team, whether it be positive and uplifting or not. They will never show favoritism, and they will be clear and honest about the ways in which they delegate work, assign projects and promote people. Whilst you don't have to be a workaholic to be a great leader, you should make your presence felt in the office. In short, respected leaders take care not to appear hypocritical. If you expect your team to uphold values of transparency, for example, you cannot afford to be anything less than scrupulous when making expenses claims. Act in an ethical manner and this will show through in your demeanor. In addition, it's less stressful to do the right thing in the first place than it is to try and get away with bad behavior – you will get found out one day!

Principle 2: Understand the importance of non-verbal communication. Learn to read body language and employ it to positive effect.

From the moment your team members first meet you, they will be forming judgments about you. This is natural – as humans, we judge one another all the time. However, in this particular situation the stakes for you are high, because it is hard to change peoples' first impressions and it is difficult to manage a team who don't trust you. As their leader, you want them to judge you favorably. Fortunately, you can use your body language to communicate that you are worthy of their confidence and respect.

Even if you feel nervous, make an effort to stand up straight. Imagine that there is an invisible cord running vertically from the top of your head to the ceiling and that it is pulling your head upwards so that you appear relaxed yet confident. Drop your shoulders and minimize unnecessary hand movements, as this will make you appear nervous. Make it your goal that the first time every member of your team sees you for the first time that you are smile. Don't grin like an idiot, but make an effort to relax the muscles around your mouth and jaw as you greet everyone, shaking their hands firmly but briefly. Avoid adopting submissive or defensive body language such as crossing or folding your limbs, or looking down at the floor. You have been appointed to lead, so act like it!

Principle 3: Take a sincere interest in your team members as individual people, not just employees.

The issue of whether employees should be friends with their managers is never going to die – some people believe that the best teams are on friendly terms with one another, whereas at the other end of the spectrum, others believe that managers should maintain a lot of emotional distance from those they supervise. However, it isn't controversial to say that most people appreciate being seen as individuals who have meaningful lives outside of the workplace. You won't be supervising many people who enjoy being seen as organizational drones!

Therefore, it is a good idea to make a point of paying attention to any information your team members share about themselves from the beginning. Also be sure to pay attention to any obvious visual cues – does anyone have a photo of their young children on their desk? They probably wouldn't mind if you asked after their family every now and again. Is there anyone who regularly brings in books or baked goods into the office for everyone else to enjoy in the break room? These sorts of people usually respond positively to a few questions about their hobbies and interests. Even if you couldn't care less about angel food cake recipes, it's part of your job as a leader to demonstrate that you acknowledge that everyone has a life outside of work.

Principle 4: Show that you are human too.

Remote, aloof leaders who act in such a way that suggests they are somehow 'above' everyone else are not popular. Can leading in a 'transactional' way – in which you are concerned with outcomes rather than values and teambuilding – work? Of course. However, those who aim for a 'transformational' leadership approach are more likely to develop an atmosphere of cooperation, joy and progress at work. It sounds much more relaxing, doesn't it?

Of course you need to maintain an appropriate level of professionalism at work. However, never allowing yourself to have a slightly grumpy morning or laugh at a joke told by a colleague will not endear you to anyone. Again, it can be helpful to think about the leaders you most admire. In all probability, you most admire those who are focused on their work but at the same time are unafraid to break loose once in a while.

Principle 5: Show sincere appreciation and praise.

Whether they show it or not, everyone likes to be appreciated for the work that they do. This is true even if the person in question doesn't enjoy their job, or would rather be working in a different field altogether. It doesn't matter – we all have a basic need to be needed and wanted.

Take advantage of this simple piece of psychology by giving out praise whenever it is deserved. Of course, you should never praise people just for the sake of it, as this will only earn you a reputation as insincere or desperate to win the affection of your team. Instead, aim simply to vocalize every positive thought you have about your team's performance or efforts. It's surprisingly easy to let people go unacknowledged. A simple 'Great job!' or

'Nicely done' delivered with a quick smile can make someone's afternoon.

Giving praise also conveys to others that you are essentially a positive person who likes to see the best in every situation, and this is a very attractive quality in a leader. Employees like to be lead by someone who can be relied upon to see the best in every situation. If your team doesn't already have an incentive structure in place, why not implement one? This can be as simple as an 'Employee Of The Month' certificate or a more elaborate program consisting of financial or material incentives for great performance.

Principle 6: Show that you can be flexible.

It can be tempting, especially if you are new to an organization, to dive straight in and try to implement your ideas. This is a mistake. Remember that even when you have been hired to make a drastic difference to an existing team, you are going to be working with people who have done things in a certain way for a while, perhaps even years! Therefore, it is important to introduce changes in a sensitive way. This sets a precedent, establishing yourself as a leader who has high standards but avoids expecting miracles.

In practice, this means upholding the previously mentioned values of honesty and transparency. Everyone will be expecting you to make changes, but it is important that you explain your reasoning and processes via the appropriate channels. During times of intense change, hold weekly staff meetings in which you outline both what you are doing and why you're doing it. This is preferable to simply writing and sending emails, because in person you have the benefit of monitoring everyone's body language. This is valuable, because although it is easy to say 'Yes' or 'Great idea, boss!' in writing, it is harder to fake genuine enthusiasm in person. Therefore, holding meetings will help you better gauge everyone's reactions to your suggestions.

Another aspect of remaining flexible is to be open and receptive to feedback from those you lead. This is a significant topic in its own right, so we'll be returning to the subject at several points later in the book. For now, it's enough to say that people value leaders who can admit when they are wrong and look to others for guidance and support.

Principle 7: Keep your team challenged but not overstretched.

Along with feeling needed, human beings crave stimulation. This will vary from person to person – some seem to have a higher boredom threshold than others – but as a rule, if you want a happy team then you need to assign them sufficient work that they are engaged, but not so much that they become burned out.

This may be the hardest of the principles to implement, because it requires you to become familiar with the limitations and special talents of each team member. You can gain a head start here by asking your new employer for files or notes on each employee. If you are given the opportunity to hold a 'meet the team' meeting prior to your contract beginning, use it as your first chance to understand where their strengths and weaknesses lie. Who is the strongest communicator in the team? Who appears to be the best organized? Who works best under pressure?

Within the first few weeks, you will quickly come to appreciate how your team is currently managing their workload. It may be beneficial to ask each person to note down, for a few days, how they spend their time. If they feel overstretched, you can use this information to prioritize their tasks and work with them to establish a more realistic schedule.

On the other hand, you may find that you have among your team those whose talents are not utilized properly. Such people may perform adequately, but appear under stimulated. This is where you must exercise your responsibility as a manager to balance your subordinates' workload. In such a case, you should consider challenging them by asking them to assume responsibility for a new project or to help an overstretched co-worker.

The Most Common Leadership Communication Obstacles

Strong communication skills are vital to successful leadership. Unfortunately, there are certain pitfalls that can cause problems for both experienced and new managers. This chapter will take you through the most common obstacles of which leaders must be aware if they are to communicate their messages and instructions to people they lead.

Overuse of business jargon.

Always aim to be clear and direct when talking to others. Do not be tempted to use corporate buzzwords or phrases if they are unnecessary. If you have to use a specific term that might be unfamiliar to the average person on the street, make sure you define it clearly at the outset and then return to plain English as soon as possible.

Using business jargon does not impress people – at least, not the kind of people you ought to care about impressing. Instead, it makes you appear unnecessarily aloof and can even create the impression that you are 'hiding' behind long words rather than addressing the issues directly. This does not inspire confidence in you as a leader.

Lack of confidence and certainty.

You must communicate confidently if you want your team to take you seriously. If you aren't sure of your own objectives, others will pick up on this and lose trust in you. Before attending a meeting or writing an email, ask yourself what it is that you are trying to convey in your message. Don't be afraid to state exactly what the purpose of your communication is – e.g., 'I've called this meeting about our new supplier this morning, because I'm concerned that the time required to manage their requirements may cost us valuable resources that are allocated to other projects.' If this sounds obvious, do it anyway. It's always better to risk over-simplification than leave people wondering what on earth you are saying, or even worse, why you are bothering to talk about it at all.

Insensitivity to cultural differences.

We live in an increasingly globalized world, and diversity in the workplace is rightly celebrated and encouraged. This can, however, present certain problems for leaders. To give a simple example, consider traditional cultural differences between western and Asian countries. In the former group of societies, a direct and individual-centered leadership style has been traditionally favored. However, in other cultures, it is considered rude to question your 'superiors' or elders, which may mean that team members from other cultures may be hesitant to offer you anything remotely resembling criticism or negative feedback. Tension may also arise if you and a co-worker are from very different social classes, or if there is a wide age gap.

There is no need to be pessimistic about differences, as in reality many people communicate well despite coming from dissimilar backgrounds. However, it is important to be aware that miscommunication can and does occur because of these issues. The solution is to keep your expectations clear regarding 'how we do things around here,' and keep these expectations for everyone. Don't draw attention to cultural differences, but aim to keep your language as accessible to as many groups of people as possible. For example, avoid in-jokes or particular cultural references that some team members may not pick up on. If you find yourself working regularly with people whose culture is alien to you, consider seeking advice from HR as to how you can avoid potentially awkward miscommunications.

Picking the wrong medium for your message.

Routine updates can be given via email, but significant information ought to be delivered in person or over the phone and then acknowledged with a follow-up email. Following an important in-person conversation, send the other party a message containing the key points raised. End the email by stating that if the other person has no objections, you assume that the email represents a valid record of the conversation. Make sure that you obtain a 'Read' receipt for the message, and keep a printed copy if the matter is especially sensitive. This can prevent disputes later.

Jumping to conclusions based on single incidents or isolated pieces of body language.

Have you ever noticed someone yawn whilst you were talking, and felt annoyed as a result? It's easy to notice a single element of someone's body language and draw negative inferences. You must resist the urge to do this, as it can result in you feeling unnecessarily anxious or angry towards your team. Remember that yes, someone could be yawning in a meeting because they are bored, but they could also be tired or coming down with a cold. Pay attention to their broader pattern of behaviors instead. If a co-worker is generally respectful and hardworking, don't waste time becoming annoyed because they looked tired or slightly withdrawn one afternoon.

The 'Chinese Whispers' phenomenon.

If you have some vital news to impart, make sure that you are giving the information directly to everyone concerned. Do not trust that others can be trusted to pass it on with absolute accuracy! Whilst it is important to trust those directly below you in the chain of command, take the time to communicate important news and information personally. This should be done in person and then backed up by an email trail. Otherwise, you run the risk of others misinterpreting what you say, and confusion may result. In the early days of your management role, as you are still gauging the reliability and personalities of your team members, remember that the more direct you can be, the better.

Assuming that 'no questions' means 'everyone has understood.'

Have you ever been in a meeting, listened closely to what the leader was saying, yet still felt clueless when you left? Perhaps you were too embarrassed to admit that you needed further clarification, and didn't raise your hand or voice to ask questions.

It's important that you as a leader remember that just because people don't ask you any questions in a meeting, it doesn't mean that everyone has understood you perfectly. Some people might be convinced that they are the only one in the room who doesn't understand and be hesitant to ask you to explain a concept for a second or third time. The fear of looking stupid or incompetent is strong in most people.

Ideally, you will have created a supportive, positive environment in which people feel able to admit that they don't know everything, but this will take time to build that trust. In the meantime, make sure that everyone has ample opportunity to provide you with feedback or ask questions. This means allowing plenty of time at the end of meetings for questions, but it also means replying to emails promptly from the beginning of your time as a leader (so that people feel as though they can email you with questions), being regularly seen around the office (so that people can approach you in person), and always treating people with respect (so they never have to fear being mocked for asking questions).

Failing to make your presence felt.

No-one likes to be around an unreasonable, overly-grumpy or demanding leader. This is where the stereotype of the employees who cheer every time they hear that their boss will be out of the office. However, if you attempt to implement the leadership advice contained within this book, this won't apply to you! Instead, your team will actually appreciate the opportunity to see you on a regular basis.

Even if you have a private office, park in a different area of the car park to everyone else, and have a PA who guards your diary, make the effort to be accessible. Call into everyone's office as often as your schedule reasonably allows. Give your team plenty of opportunity to tell you, in person, how their work is going. Just because we now live in an age of digital communication doesn't mean that people have lost their deep-seated appreciation for in-person contact. Furthermore, demonstrating that you are willing to make the effort to see everyone proves that you value everyone's time and contribution. It will also allow you to spot problems as they arise, which can ultimately save a lot of time and agony down the road.

How To Say What You Mean And Still Have People Admire You

There's no getting away from it – sometimes as a leader you will have to say things that aren't going to be well-received. You may have to announce budget cuts, pay freezes, or break the news that a particular project will require everyone to put in some hours over the weekend. On other occasions, you will have to voice your disagreement with other peoples' opinions. From time to time, you may even find yourself in direct conflict with others. Remember that this is normal – in fact, an organization in which everyone gets along perfectly well all the time is to be viewed with suspicion, because this either indicates a culture of fear in which no-one dare voice their opinions, or a culture of conformity in which people are hired on the basis that they will fit in and cause minimum disturbance. Neither of these scenarios give an organization room to grow and innovate. To some degree, you should welcome an occasional argument or heated discussion!

Here's some more good news - there are techniques you can use to deliver difficult messages in a no-nonsense but humane manner that mean people will admire you even when you are saying things they don't want to hear. If you are still hesitant when it comes to saying what you really mean, remember that people find it hard to respect those who shy away from challenging issues. Even if it is tough to stand up for your own beliefs and opinions, living with integrity will yield you the most respect in the long run, both from others and from yourself.

Lay the groundwork by upholding the right values.

We've already addressed how important it is to maintain your integrity and transparency as a leader. Do this and you will already have prepared other people for those times when you need to deliver bad news or disagree with them. Why? Because if you have already gained a reputation for being open and honest, people won't be too surprised when you say exactly what you think and mean.

Explain your entire thought process when putting forward your point of view.

Don't leave anyone feeling confused. If you need to tell your team about a recent decision you have had to make, an opinion you hold that goes against the majority, or a significant change in policy or procedure, be sure to take it slow and start from the beginning. Simply summarizing what you believe is not enough – to convince people that you are worthy of being listened to or that your decision-making skills are sound, it is vital that you provide insight into your thought processes.

For instance, explain how and why you came to end a major contract with a certain supplier rather than just calling everyone into a room and announcing that the organization will no longer be working with them. When you take the time and effort to explain the reasons behind your actions, people will respect and trust you. They will perceive that you regard them as intelligent people who need and appreciate insight into company decisions. Taking this approach also prevents toxic, timewasting office gossip and reduces feelings of panic in more insecure team members.

Use the Sandwich Technique.

If you find yourself in a position whereby you feel as though you must disagree with a co-worker's suggestion or launch an objection, try the sandwich technique. Essentially, begin by offering a brief positive comment, followed by your main point, finishing off with another positive remark. For example, you may say something like this: .I think you've shown a lot of thought there into how you've planned out our strategy for the next quarter. But I'd like to suggest that we need to make re-organizing our logistics department our main priority here, and I don't see that well-represented in these plans. I really am impressed by the detail here, though.. This strategy makes it less likely that you will irritate other people, and shows respect for their beliefs and efforts.

Give people the respect of breaking bad news in person.

This tip shouldn't require much by way of explanation. If you need to reduce someone's hours, subject them to disciplinary action or let them go from the company, always do so in person and in a private room if possible. Even if you are releasing someone from the company, they may still tell those left behind if you were insensitive in doing so, and this may harm your reputation. Put yourself in their position and treat them as you would want to be treated.

Remain positive even in the face of bad news. Reframe it as an opportunity to do something different, new, or better.

There may be instances in your management career when you have to break terrible news to your team, for instance in the event of company closure or the passing of a co-worker. In such cases, attempting to put a positive spin on the news would be crass and insensitive.

However, much of the time, there is usually some kind of upside to be found if you look hard enough. This is a valuable skill to learn, because people like and respect leaders who acknowledge bad news yet also encourage their team to regard it as a learning experience. Before calling a meeting or sending out a message detailing negative news, try to find at least one somewhat positive outcome. For instance, although your team may have lost a contract, this may free up their time to make another project especially good.

Resist the temptation to overshare.

There's nothing wrong with a leader who feels passionate about their work and reacts to major events with strong feelings. However, it is important that you do not share absolutely everything that you think and feel. As a general rule, tell people what they need to know and what you would like to know were you in their position, but no more than that. Under no circumstance should you disclose any confidential information that those above you would rather not become common knowledge. No matter how much you trust and like your team, you can bet that somehow, you will be identified as the source of the information leak.

Practice the tough stuff out loud, alone, to perfect your tone and body language.

Public speaking is hard work for most people, and if you need to address a crowd it can be absolutely nerve-wracking, particularly if you need to impart bad news. If you haven't engaged in much public speaking prior to your first leadership role, now might be a good point to seek out training or classes to help you develop this skill. Do this early on, before you run into your first crisis — and it's inevitable that you will, as life is unpredictable — and you'll feel better-equipped to handle the tough times ahead.

If you have to make a presentation or give a talk in which you will be required to deliver bad news, practice first. Lock the door, stand in front of a full-length mirror, and look at your body language. Check that your posture is straight, that your hands aren't twisting together or pulling at your clothing, and that you are looking straight ahead. Practice addressing the back of the room and projecting your voice by speaking from your diaphragm rather than the back of your throat. Attending a group such as Toastmaster's International can help you to perfect your technique, as can any public speaking or media training offered by your employer. You never know until you ask, so if you frequently find yourself becoming nervous when talking to groups, why not ask your manager if there are opportunities available to help you improve in this area? It isn't a sign of weakness to say that you need help. On the contrary, it shows that you are willing to take an honest inventory of your strengths and weaknesses, which makes you a desirable employee and leader.

What If People Disagree With You?

At some point - in all probability, it will come sooner rather than later — you are going to come up against people who disagree with you. This is something you need to get used to, especially if you work with a large or diverse team of people. Knowing how to handle negative feedback and differences of opinion is an essential skill for any leader.

Realize that they might be right, so hear them out.

When someone disagrees with you, is your default assumption that you must be in the right and they in the wrong? If so, you need to adjust your attitude right now. You cannot expect to be right on every occasion — no-one is perfect or superhuman. In other words, when someone pushes back against you, you ought to assume that they may have a point. They may not necessarily be completely correct in their assessment, but be prepared to concede that you should listen to what they have to say. This is particularly true if you are new to the role or to an organization. Do not dismiss someone else's opinions simply because they are less experienced, more junior, or younger than you.

If you find yourself agreeing with what they are saying, don't be afraid to acknowledge this openly.

Even if their view is nonsense, think of your reputation before you overreact.

All well and good, you may think, but what if the other person in question really is wrong, or is known to spout a lot of nonsense? You should listen to them anyway, and take them seriously. Why? Quite simply, you don't want a reputation as someone who casts aside the views of those they lead. You want a reputation as a leader who is willing to stand firm in their beliefs but who also welcomes points of view that differ from their own.

Therefore, it is important that you grant the person who is disagreeing with you sufficient time to air their grievance. Handle this in the most discreet and professional manner possible. For example, it is always better to conduct sensitive discussions behind closed doors rather than conduct a shouting match in the middle of an open-plan office. Setting up a meeting with a formal beginning and end time also allows both of you to prepare what you will say in advance, which ensures that everyone gets the opportunity to feel heard.

See disagreements as a sign of success.

Don't be surprised or upset when people push back against your ideas – it's a sign of a positive workplace when people can respectfully disagree with their line manager. It doesn't mean you have failed. It just means you have final responsibility to take into account all the available information and come to a sensible, well-informed decision. Employees who can challenge their managers can even save lives in some situations. They should feel able to point out impending catastrophes and suggest better, safer ways of conducting organizational activities. So make you stay open to what others say, and don't let your pride get in the way.

Your own manager, if they understand what it truly means to be a great leader, ought to be impressed that you expect your team members to disagree with you from time to time. They will feel reassured that you aren't dangerously arrogant

Get a record of the conversation, and ask for witness statements if applicable.

In most cases, disagreements are low-level and can be sorted out with a few minutes of constructive conversation. However, you may occasionally be drawn into a more heated argument with a coworker. If this is the case, you need to focus on three things:

1. Remaining calm;
2. Reminding yourself of your objectives;
3. Obtaining a record of events and words exchanged.

Remaining calm comes with practice. It's about keeping your eyes on the bigger picture. Remember that even full-on rows probably won't matter a few weeks from now, and this time next year they will be a distant memory. Don't let yourself become emotionally tangled in the moment. If you need to excuse yourself from the room for a few moments to go to the bathroom, do so. You will win the respect of others by demonstrating that you understand the need to approach conflict from a calm perspective.

Next, remind yourself of your objectives – you have a particular problem that needs solving, and you need to reach some kind of resolution with the minimum of hurt feelings and injury to work relationships. Remind yourself that any work-related argument is much larger than the parties concerned; your primary motive ought to be furthering the aims and success of your organization. Try to shift your focus away from how annoyed or angry you feel with the co-worker in question and instead make sure that you try to secure the best possible outcome for the good of the company. Remind yourself that whilst it's wonderful to be liked by your team, good leadership is not a popularity contest and you are not going to make friends with everyone.

Finally, always get a record of significant conflicts. Following a heated or controversial exchange, write down your version of events and send it via email to all parties involved. Indicate that you felt the debate was worth recording for everyone's sake, and unless they write back to you giving their thoughts to the contrary, you will assume that your account will stand as an accurate reference should any further problems arise. Doing this establishes your reputation as someone who takes disagreements seriously, and it also allows you to cover your own back to some extent should a member of your team later attempt to approach a higher-level manager or launch a formal complaint against you. Although most people will not want to drag out conflict longer than is necessary, there are a few individuals within every large organization who will gladly make trouble wherever possible. It is vital that you understand how important it is to protect yourself from them.

Consider the stakeholders and broader political implications.

Sometimes it is not politically wise to argue, even if you know that you are right. Why? Well, sometimes you need to consider the long-term implications of siding with a particular person, especially if the matter is somewhat trivial, and then use this knowledge to work out how you ought to approach the situation. For example, you may disagree with one of your co-workers, but is your boss or client likely to side with this other party? If this is the case, it may be worth going along with their point of view rather than risk causing unnecessary tensions or rifts.

Bear in mind that compromising can give you leverage later to get you what you want.

Most people think in terms of reciprocation – if you grant them a favor, they often feel beholden to you. In other words, people generally operate on a 'tit for tat' basis. This means that if you choose to compromise with a co-worker, even when you don't have to, they will probably feel as though they 'owe you' a favor later on. Wise leaders use this piece of psychology to their advantage. If you make a point of 'giving in' on relatively minor issues to keep the peace, you can draw upon the store of goodwill you will build up later on when you need something from the person in question. This may sound manipulative, but it is a basic principle of human relationships that most people can and do keep score to some degree. Make sure that you aren't asking for significantly more compromise than you are willing to grant yourself.

Don't just impose your will, unless it's an emergency – people don't easily forgive or forget a tyrant.

If the dispute is ongoing or looks likely to trigger a major rift, schedule a proper meeting to drill down to the real source of the disagreement. Do this as soon as possible. Unless there is a true crisis at work or your team is in urgent need of someone to wade in and restore order, resist the urge to impose your will on people and tell them to obey you purely on the grounds that you are the leader and they are your subordinates.

Such a brutal approach works well in times of emergency and can earn you a grudging respect, but it isn't the best method for long-term engagement and happy working relationships. Make your standard leadership style collaborative and flexible instead of tyrannical, if for no other reason than it gets seriously tiring to be loud and forceful all the time.

What To Do With Really Annoying Co-workers

You will quickly learn, as a leader, that not everyone you work with is going to like you, respect you, or share your views. We've already looked at how to handle conflict, but what about people who are simply, well, annoying? Here are a few hints on how to handle certain types of personality you may come across in the workplace.

Consider whether their attitude is situation or person-specific.

If you find yourself frequently coming into conflict with a particular person, your first priority should be to ascertain whether it's you they have a problem with, or whether they behave in a similar way to everyone they meet. Notice how they interact with others. You may find that this person has an attitude problem and this discovery may help you to take their behavior less personally.

However, if it's just you they have a problem with, rejoice! Why? Because if you can change your relationship with them, you've solved the problem. Follow the steps in this book and you will make enough of a positive impression on other people that you are likely to earn at least a basic level of respect from this person over time. If not, see it as a lesson in a harsh management reality – that not everyone will grant you the respect you deserve.

If you get the impression that an annoying co-worker or team member is unhappy, make every effort to understand why.

If a member of your team is irritatingly glum or pedantic, schedule a frank discussion about their attitude. Explain it isn't just you it's affecting- it's their own happiness, the other members of their team, and ultimately the performance of the organization as a whole. Rather than treating their problem as an issue within themselves that needs to be fixed, treat their unhappiness as an issue that you can both work jointly to solve. Explain that you know it isn't realistic to expect everyone to enjoy their work and show an outstanding attitude all of the time, but you both have a common interest in enjoying your jobs and adding value to the company. Don't forget to document everything.

Sometimes a single change can stimulate personal growth.

Sometimes people become bored and take it out on others because they are stagnating. Could this be true for that annoying team member? Perhaps they need a change in their routine, some new responsibility, or a new challenge.

Try the broken record technique.

If you are unlucky enough to work with someone who raises the same issues over and over again or who asks you inappropriate questions, use the Broken Record technique. This entails choosing a 'default response' and repeating it every time they trot out the same old question. For example, if you have a team member who continually asks you about the vacation policy, even if it is not your responsibility, try saying something like 'I'm afraid HR is your best bet for that, not me.' Eventually, they will get the message and bother somebody else.

If you have a practical joker in the office, try to channel their efforts elsewhere.

Some people are well-intentioned but nonetheless manage to irritate everyone around them. This is particularly common in 'office jokers,' who seem to make it their mission in life to play pranks or act in a silly fashion as often as possible. To some extent, they should be tolerated – they can add character to a workplace! However, if their antics are having a detrimental effect on the team's productivity, they need to be bought in line. Try a two-pronged approach. Have a one-to-one discussion with them and underline the fact that you appreciate the levity they bring to the workplace, but that they need to tone down their behavior.

At the same time, give them an outlet to channel their energies. Perhaps you could make them responsible for the work socials, for instance. Alternatively, give them some additional work-related challenges that will keep their brains occupied. These sorts of people are often creative and you can make good use of this energy.

If someone thinks they know best all the time, give them a chance to prove it and call their bluff.

If you have to manage a chronic whiner or somebody who subtly suggests that they could do everything better than you if only they were given the opportunity, call their bluff. Make it a point to ask them what they think about difficult issues, and ask them to explain in detail how they would handle a situation. Their responses may be hard to listen to, but they may realize once they are forced to reason a situation aloud, that you are the manager for a reason!

If someone persistently disagrees with your thinking on certain issues but fails to offer constructive suggestions, start asking them for brief written reports containing their input on particular situations. They will soon learn not to casually assert that they could do a better job, or that they have all the answers.

When To Argue
And When To Let It Go

We've already taken a look at how to handle disagreements and how to deal with annoying co-workers, but sometimes you need to ask yourself whether an issue is really worth bothering with in the first place. If you find yourself frequently drawn into conflicts and disagreements – or having to sort them out between two or more of your team members – it may be time to consider whether you are granting too much time to the wrong kinds of issue. Consider the following points when you sense an argument brewing at work.

Sometimes it's better to let someone make a minor mistake by themselves, as long as they have the ability to clear up the mess!

Is a member of your team insistent that they be allowed to do something a certain way, even though it is plain to other people that they are setting themselves up for a fall? One way to handle such a situation is to grant them the chance to teach themselves a lesson. If possible, tell them that you disagree with how they want to handle the scenario, but that you want to let them learn from their own experiences. Take a deep breath and let them make their own mistakes. Note that you should never do this if the stakes are high, but that allowing someone to make their own errors can be a valuable teaching tool.

Of course, if it turns out that they were right, don't be too proud to admit that they have done a good job. Be humble!

Don't take the fall for someone else.

Although a good leader protects their team to some extent and accepts ultimate responsibility for their outcomes, there is little sense in risking your own reputation for the sake of keeping the peace and going along with a suggestion you feel to be wrong. If someone else's stubborn nature will cost you personally, state your case and then put your foot down.

Ask yourself whether the issue will cease to matter within a week or month.

If the answer is 'No, it won't matter to anyone,' then it probably isn't worth arguing about. Smooth things over as quickly as possible and move onto more important topics. Your time is a valuable commodity, and it makes no sense to argue about petty issues when you have bigger priorities on which to focus. Model this attitude for your team, and they will learn where to direct their own energies.

Sometimes you have to let other people disagree – from separate rooms.

Sometimes it is appropriate to let two of your team members engage in healthy disagreement. However, if they start calling one another names or dragging up issues from the past, it's time to step in and force a truce. This may require you to send one off to engage in an unrelated work task, or even to ask them to sit in separate rooms for a while. If your office atmosphere is informal and the issue is relatively petty, try to gently point out that they are silly to argue this particular point. This may be enough to help them realize that their time would be better spent elsewhere.

Try to foresee issues that may cause conflict ahead of time, so you can anticipate how best to diffuse the situation. For instance, if you know that two of your team members are likely to get into a disagreement at a particular meeting, you could have a discreet conversation with them both prior to the event and state that whilst you respect that they have a difference of opinion, you are expecting that they will both agree to act like mature adults and share in their commitment to act in the best interests of the company.

Consider the context.

If you catch yourself feeling especially irritable one day for no apparent reason, stay on your guard so as to make sure you don't get into unnecessary arguments. As a rule, do not argue when you are unusually busy, when you are especially tired, or first thing on a Monday morning - this will set an unpleasant tone for the rest of the week.

How To Finally Start Remembering Names

If you manage a large team, you may be required to learn many names in a relatively short space of time. Many leaders find this hard, so here are a few hints that may help!

Put photos of your team members in a convenient file.

Most organizations keep official photographs on file for all employees. Print out an A4 sheet of these photos, with accompanying names, and keep it close to hand. Spend a couple of minutes per day studying this sheet until you learn who's who.

Use their first name in conversation.

Using someone's first name in a greeting and then a couple of times during a conversation will help consolidate it in your memory as your brain will hear the word used in a real-life context. Don't over-use their name – that sounds odd or creepy – but be sure to include it in every meaningful interaction at least once.

Get to know your team as people.

The greater your appreciation of your team members as people, the more readily you will remember their names because they will seem more real and important to you. Make a point of asking after their children, families or about a particular hobby that seems important to them.

If your personality and that of your organization seem suitable, suggest everyone wear name tags for a few days or introduces them whenever they talk to you.

If you are new to an organization and are faced with the task of learning a lot of names in a short amount of time, take a brazen approach and ask everyone to wear small name tags for your first few days. Alternatively, if this tactic isn't quite in keeping with your personality, politely request that everyone introduces themselves by name for the first fortnight you are in your new role.

How To Give Valuable Feedback

As a leader, you will be required to give feedback at regular intervals to all members of your team. This can be rewarding when things are going well, but tough when you need to make suggestions as to how people can improve. Read on for a few hints on giving better, more helpful feedback.

Use the Sandwich Technique.

As mentioned previously, the Sandwich Technique is a way of making critical or negative feedback or news more palatable through the delivery of positive reinforcement just prior and after the main content.

When giving feedback, always begin and end by making a positive statement of some kind. For example, you could praise someone's effort on, and attitude towards, a project even if the outcome was not satisfactory.

Focus on goals as well as past performance.

Whether giving good, neutral or negative feedback, move the discussion towards goals as soon as possible. For those who are performing well, goals give them further direction and incentive to behave in a productive fashion. For those who are underperforming, goals help prevent feelings of hopelessness and helplessness. Never allow someone to go away from a performance review or progress meeting without a good idea of where they should be going next. A lack of focus and certainty will reduce any employee's motivation and lower their performance.

When you take on a leadership role, you will be instructed to follow a particular feedback framework, if your role entails delivering it on a regular basis. It's a good idea to follow the company's prescribed procedures, but if you detect any weaknesses, don't hesitate to approach someone in charge of feedback at HR and politely raise the issue.

Remember the basic guidelines behind all good goal-setting: remember the acronym SMART:

Specific: Goals should address behaviors and targets that can be pinpointed. For example, 'Improve output by 25% within six weeks' is specific, whereas 'improve output soon' is not specific enough.

Measureable: Goals should result in outcomes that can be objectively measured. For example, 'Be in the office on time 100% of the time within the next two weeks.' This is measurable because time can be objectively measured!

Achievable: Goals should actually be feasible.

Relevant: Goals should relate to broader aims and objectives. There is no point in setting a goal if it will not help someone fulfil their job role appropriately.

Time-bound: Goals should always be placed a time context. Goals can span timeframes from days to years, but it is important that the person striving to achieve it have a deadline or similar with which to work.

Focus on the behaviours, not the person.

If you are facing the unpleasant task of admonishing an employee for poor performance or inappropriate behaviour, keep your conversation focused on what they have actually done (or not done), rather than picking holes in their personality. Although it is hard, try to distinguish the person from the way in which they are acting. For example, if a team member is frequently late, stick to the facts when explaining how they need to change, rather than blasting them for their 'sloppy attitude.' Make it clear that you require them to meet certain standards – to be in the office for 8.30am every day unless they are ill or ask permission beforehand to come in later – or else there will be tangible consequences (e.g. a formal written warning).

Regular feedback is important.

If your company doesn't already have a procedure in place by which regular feedback is delivered to employees, make a priority to have one up and running as soon as possible. This can be as simple as a six-month review with a standardised questionnaire, or something more elaborate such as a '360' feedback system in which the employee, their colleagues, and their manager all provide feedback which is then consolidated into a single interview. Ask your peers with similar responsibilities to your own how they approach feedback with their team members. You can save yourself a lot of hassle, time, trial and error by learning from those who have been with the company for longer and understand its culture.

Roadtest your feedback style.

Ask a trusted colleague or friend to give you an honest assessment of your feedback style. Ask them to pretend that they are under your supervision, and that you are giving them feedback. Show them how you deliver positive, neutral and negative feedback. Ask them to comment on your choice of words, pacing, and body language. Ask them to imagine how they would feel leaving the meeting if they were in the position of someone in your team. You may find that you need to communicate more clearly, or perhaps adopt a more encouraging tone of voice. It can be easy to assume that other people infer from us exactly what we are intending to communicate, but often this isn't the case! Minimize the risk of this happening by role playing first.

Conclusion

Thank you for choosing and downloading this book! With your newfound knowledge and practical tips to try, you are well-placed to fully develop your leadership potential. Remember that learning to lead well is a lifelong project. Good luck, and here's to your success.

Finally, if you enjoyed this book, would you be kind enough to leave a review for this book on Amazon? Thank you.

Lightning Source UK Ltd.
Milton Keynes UK
UKOW06f1855100716

278050UK00010B/349/P